AF726022

Laura Mannering is a solicitor advocate and partner at Edwards Duthie Shamash Solicitors with over fifteen years of experience specialising in Court of Protection and Community Care law. Laura is also an Accredited Legal Representative (ALR) under the Law Society Mental Capacity Accreditation Scheme. Laura has a particular interest in cases in the Court of Protection representing vulnerable adults in proceedings relating to their mental capacity and best interests in respect of issues concerning their residence, care, contact with particular individuals, foreign travel, contraception and engaging in sexual relations and consent to marriage, as well as cases involving decisions about serious medical treatment.

Laura was instructed in the matters of Kent County Council v P (by her litigation friend the Official Solicitor) v NHS Kent and Medway Commissioning Group (formerly NHS South Kent CCG) [2022] EWCOP 3 and Esper v NHS NW London ICB (Appeal : Anonymity in Committal Proceedings), Re (Rev1) [2023] EWCOP 29 (10 July 2023), both of which are considered in this guide.

A Practical Guide to Privacy, Transparency, Reporting Restrictions and Closed Hearings in the Court of Protection

A Practical Guide to Privacy, Transparency, Reporting Restrictions and Closed Hearings in the Court of Protection

Laura Mannering

Partner, Edwards Duthie Shamash Solicitors

MA (Oxon)

Law Brief Publishing

© Laura Mannering

All rights reserved. No part of this publication may be reproduced, stored in a retrieval system, or transmitted, in any form or by any means, electronic, mechanical, photocopying, recording or otherwise, without the prior permission of the publisher.

Excerpts from judgments and statutes are Crown copyright. Any Crown Copyright material is reproduced with the permission of the Controller of OPSI and the King's Printer for Scotland. Some quotations may be licensed under the terms of the Open Government Licence (http://www.nationalarchives.gov.uk/doc/open-government-licence/version/3).

Cover image © iStockphoto.com/Chaz Bharj

The information in this book was believed to be correct at the time of writing. All content is for information purposes only and is not intended as legal advice. No liability is accepted by either the publisher or author for any errors or omissions (whether negligent or not) that it may contain. Professional advice should always be obtained before applying any information to particular circumstances.

Published 2024 by Law Brief Publishing, an imprint of Law Brief Publishing Ltd
30 The Parks
Minehead
Somerset
TA24 8BT

www.lawbriefpublishing.com

Paperback: 978-1-916698-42-0

This book is dedicated to my mother,
Linda, who gave me all her support always.

PREFACE

Following a transparency pilot in 2016, there has been a shift in the practice of the Court of Protection towards more hearings being heard in public although still being subject to orders restricting the information that can be shared and reported outside of those hearing.

A new Practice Direction was implemented in 2017, governing the procedure for the making of transparency orders to restrict the reporting from a public hearing and addressing the matters that the court must consider in deciding whether to deviate from the ordinary position of hearings now being in public.

The court has grappled with issues arising from the change of approach and the increase in hearings being heard in public.

There are important principles of open justice, as well as the need to uphold the freedom of the press and the Article 10 rights of the press and public to discuss matters arising from the often important and complex cases which the Court of Protection decides. These need to be balanced against the equally important Article 8 rights of both the person whom the case is about, and others involved in the proceedings.

This guide looks at the procedural rules governing the way that hearings in the Court of Protection take place, and the case law dealing with issues of privacy, reporting and transparency in respect of proceedings in the Court of Protection.

The stated law in this guide is believed to be accurate and up to date at 30 June 2024.

I would like to thank my colleagues in the Court of Protection team at Edwards Duthie Shamash for their support, and special thanks to my colleague Kris Jackson-Hughes for giving me his time to review my drafts and give me his thoughts and tips.

Laura Mannering
July 2024

CONTENTS

Introduction		1
Chapter One	The Rules and Practice Directions	5
	The general rule	5
	Public hearings	8
	Practice Direction 4C – Transparency and transparency orders	10
	Practice Direction 4A	14
	Summary	17
Chapter Two	Privacy	21
	Private hearings and reporting	21
	The balancing exercise: Article 8 ECHR v Article 10 ECHR	23
	The case law	26
	Summary	32
Chapter Three	Transparency	35
	Transparency orders - P's information	35
	Transparency orders - the information of other parties/individuals'	41
	Summary	45

Chapter Four	Lifting Reporting Restrictions	49
	Lifting the restrictions	49
	A decision not to lift the reporting restrictions	58
	Summary	60
Chapter Five	Transparency and Privacy in the Context of Committal Proceedings in the Court of Protection	63
	The Rules	63
	The case law	65
	Summary	75
Chapter Six	Transparency in the Context of Closed Proceedings	77
	The guidance	77
	The case law	78
	Summary	83
Chapter Seven	Conclusions	85

INTRODUCTION

This guide considers how the Court of Protection protects the privacy of those individuals involved in proceedings before the Court of Protection, many of whom are vulnerable, whilst balancing this with the competing interests of the public to see how important decisions are being made in the Court of Protection and how the court administers justice.

The fact that the Court of Protection can be seized with decision making in relation to an individual's health and welfare, including serious medical treatment decisions, as well as their property and financial affairs, means that the cases it deals with usually concern particularly sensitive information about the private lives of those individuals.

This guide will consider Practice Direction 4C – Transparency (PD4C), which was implemented in 2017, after a pilot scheme which trialled the opening up of hearings in the Court of Protection to observers in a way which had not routinely been done previously.

It will look at the mechanisms of PD 4C, and subsequent case law considering its application, as well as the Rules and Practice Direction applicable to hearings which remain private.

The introduction of PD 4C has enabled the court to balance the competing interests of the individual's right to privacy and the important principle of open justice.

Mr Justice Toulson articulated the established principle of open justice in the matter of *Guardian News and Media Ltd, R (on the application of) v City of Westminster Magistrates Court* [2012] EWCA Civ 420[1], at paragraph 1 of his judgment:

> *"...In a democracy, where power depends on the consent of the people governed, the answer must lie in the transparency of the legal process. Open justice lets in the light and allows the public to scrutinise the workings of the law, for better or for worse..."*

The Court of Protection is seized with decision making about individuals who have been assessed to lack mental capacity to make certain decisions about areas of their health and welfare, or property and affairs, and who therefore often will not have any control about whether proceedings about them are brought to the court and therefore potentially into the public domain.

In addition, the nature of the issues involved in proceedings in the Court of Protection means that the information which will be before the court is often deeply personal and private.

These factors must be considered in the court's decision making, when balancing the principle of open justice against the rights of the individuals whose private lives have come under scrutiny by the court.

Furthermore, the starting point for the court in proceedings in the Court of Protection is that the purpose of its jurisdiction is to protect

1 Guardian News and Media Ltd, R (on the application of) v City of Westminster Magistrates' Court [2012] EWCA Civ 420 (03 April 2012) (bailii.org)

and promote the best interests of P, and the proceedings must not become an instrument of harm to P[2].

In *Westminster City Council v Sykes* [2014] EWCOP B9 (24 February 2014)[3], District Judge Eldergill noted;

> *"there is a strong public interest in privacy. Not to allow an incapacitated person the same general right to privacy or confidentiality that we claim it for ourselves would be to discriminate against them because of their mental illness and vulnerability.*
>
> *The one, highly important, difference is that whilst in an ideal world incapacitated people would have exactly the same right to privacy and confidentiality that the rest of us enjoy, when judges make decisions for them this brings into play the competing consideration that the public ought to know how courts of law function and administer justice: what kinds of decisions they are making, the quality of those decisions, and so forth".*

This guide will therefore also look at how the court uses transparency orders made under PD 4C, to balance the Article 8 rights of those individuals involved in proceedings in the Court of Protection in order to protect their privacy, against the Article 10 rights of the press and members of the public wishing to observe and comment on the court's decision making and the principles of open justice.

---

2 Per Mr Justice Cobb at paragraph 38 of his decision in *KK v Leeds City Council* [2020] EWCOP 64

3 Westminster City Council v Sykes [2014] EWCOP B9 (24 February 2014) (bailii.org)

The following chapters will also consider the case law and the approach of the Court of Protection to deciding whether a matter should remain private, or whether it should be heard in public, as well as occasions where attendance by members of the press and/or public has been permitted but with reporting restrictions orders made to protect the individual at the heart of the case. They will also consider how and when the Court of Protection will consider lifting the anonymisation in a case, thereby allowing P (the subject of the proceedings) to be identified.

This guide will also consider committal proceedings in the Court of Protection and the different approach that applies to transparency and reporting restrictions in those proceedings, in accordance with Part 21 of the Court of Protection Rules.

Finally, this guide will look briefly at closed material and closed proceedings and how issues of privacy and the need for transparency, and the protection of the open justice principle, are reconciled in those proceedings when there is material which should not be disclosed to one or more of the parties and/or to the wider public.

CHAPTER ONE

THE RULES AND PRACTICE DIRECTIONS

The procedural rules that govern the operation of proceedings in the Court of Protection are set out in the Court of Protection Rules 2017[4] (the Rules).

The Rules have the overriding objective of enabling the court to deal with a case justly and at proportionate cost, having regard to the principles contained in the Mental Capacity Act 2005[5].

The rules on whether, and when, a hearing is to be heard in private or in public are set out in Part 4 of the Rules.

The general rule

The default position, by virtue of Rule 4.1, is that hearings in the Court of Protection are to be held in private.

> *COPR 4.1.—(1) The general rule is that a hearing is to be held in private.*

The meaning of a private hearing is defined in Rule 4.1(2).

---

4 https://www.legislation.gov.uk/uksi/2017/1035/contents

5 https://www.legislation.gov.uk/ukpga/2005/9/contents

Pursuant to Rule 4.1(2) there are restrictions on who would ordinarily be able to attend a hearing in the Court of Protection, if it is being held in private, limiting the attendance to specific individuals which includes the parties and their legal representatives, the person who is the subject of the proceedings, and any person appointed as their litigation friend or as their representative appointed under Rule 1.2 of the Rules[6].

> *COPR 4.1 – (2) A private hearing is a hearing which only the following persons are entitled to attend—*
>
> *(a) the parties;*
>
> *(b) P (whether or not a party);*
>
> *(c) any person acting in the proceedings as a litigation friend or rule 1.2 representative;*
>
> *(d) any legal representative of a person specified in any of sub-paragraphs (a) or (b); and*
>
> *(e) any court officer.*

Therefore, the starting point according to the Rules is that hearings in the Court of Protection will be held in private, with only those people identified in Rule 4.1(2) (above) being entitled to attend.

Until a pilot scheme in 2016, this was the usual position in respect of Court of Protection hearings.

---

6 Rule 1.2 addresses the participation of P in Court of Protection proceedings and provides for the appointment of an accredited legal representative or a representative to address the matters set out in section 4(6) of the Mental Capacity Act 2005.

Notwithstanding the general rule, and the default position previously being that hearings will be in private, provision is made within the Rules to widen the list of those permitted to attend a hearing in the Court of Protection.

The court has the power, by virtue of Rule 4.1(3), to make an order authorising those not listed in Rule 4.1(2) to attend a hearing, or part of it.

This means that the court can, for example, allow members of the press or other classes of person to attend a private hearing or at the very least attend part of that hearing.

Under Rule 4.1(3) the court can also makes orders to exclude people or classes of people from attending a hearing in the Court of Protection.

This gives the Court the power to both extend and limit the scope of those permitted to attend a private hearing.

Rule 4.1(3) provides:

> *COPR 4.1(3) In relation to a private hearing, the court may make an order—*
>
> *(a) authorising any person, or class of persons, to attend the hearing or a part of it; or*
>
> *(b) excluding any person, or class of persons, from attending the hearing or a part of it.*

There is an exception to the general rule in relation to committal proceedings which means that the general rule does not apply to proceedings for committal. By virtue of Rule 4.1(4):

> *(4) The general rule in paragraph (1) does not apply to a hearing for a committal order or writ of sequestration (in respect of which rule 21.27 makes provision).*

The procedure and how this is applied in committal hearings is discussed in greater depth in chapter 5 of this guide.

Public hearings

Notwithstanding the general rule in Rule 4.1, the court has powers, under Rule 4.3, to direct that a hearing be heard in public rather than private.

> *COPR 4.3.—(1) The court may make an order—*
>
> *(a) for a hearing to be held in public;*
>
> *(b) for a part of a hearing to be held in public; or*
>
> *(c) excluding any person, or class of persons, from attending a public hearing or a part of it.*

This means that a judge in the Court of Protection can disapply the general rule and instead make an order under Rule 4.3 to hold a hearing or hearings in public.

As can be seen from Rule 4.3(1)(c), there is also provision for the court to control who is permitted to attend a hearing which is being held in public.

One of the consequences of a hearing being heard in public is that anyone attending that hearing will be privy to information from within the proceedings, some of which may be very private and confidential to the person who the case is about, or to the other parties involved.

Court of Protection cases, by their nature, involve very personal issues about the lives of the individuals on whose behalf the court is seized with making decisions.

The Court of Protection has the power to control what information from the proceedings is allowed to be published. Rule 4.3(2) provides for the making of orders to limit the publication of certain information.

Rule 4.3(2) says:

> *COPR 4.3(2) Where the court makes an order under paragraph (1), it may in the same order or by a subsequent order—*
>
> *(a) impose restrictions on the publication of the identity of—*
>
> *(i) any party;*
>
> *(ii) P (whether or not a party);*
>
> *(iii) any witness; or*
>
> *(iv) any other person;*
>
> *(b) prohibit the publication of any information that may lead to any such person being identified;*
>
> *(c) prohibit the further publication of any information relating to the proceedings from such date as the court may specify; or*

> *(d) impose such other restrictions on the publication of information relating to the proceedings as the court may specify.*

Rule 4.3(3) allows for the court, by way of a practice direction, to set out the circumstances in which the court will make an order under Rule 4.3(1) i.e. that a hearing should be heard in public.

Rule 4.3(3) provides:

> *(3) A practice direction may provide for circumstances in which the court will ordinarily make an order under paragraph (1), and for the terms of the order under paragraph (2) which the court will ordinarily make in such circumstances.*

These kinds of orders, known as transparency orders, are now made by the court in proceedings which are being heard in public, where the court wishes to control the information that is to be published or discussed in the public domain.

<u>Practice Direction 4C – Transparency and transparency orders</u>

Practice Direction 4C – Transparency[7], has been in effect since 1 December 2017.

This practice direction was introduced following a pilot of a transparency scheme, which commenced on 29 January 2016.

Under the pilot scheme hearings were held in public, with orders being made for restrictions on reporting to ensure the anonymity of

7 https://www.judiciary.uk/wp-content/uploads/2022/09/pd-4c-transparency-1.pdf

the person the case was about, 'P' and, where appropriate, other persons.

Following the pilot scheme, PD 4C was implemented.

Paragraph 1.2 of PD 4C provides that this will apply to hearings in all proceedings except applications for a committal order.

Paragraph 2.1 of PD 4C provides that the ordinary position is now that hearings will be held in public i.e. without an application having to be made for a public hearing; with a transparency order being made to control the information that is permitted to be reported or published or discussed outside of the proceedings.

PD 4C:

> *2.1 – The court will ordinarily (and so without any application being made)—*
>
> *(a) make an order under rule 4.3(1)(a) that any attended hearing shall be in public; and*
>
> *(b) in the same order, impose restrictions under rule 4.3(2) in relation to the publication of information about the proceedings.*

Paragraph 2.2 defines an "attended hearing". It says that except where a practice direction provides otherwise, an "attended hearing" means a hearing where one or more of the parties to the proceedings have been invited to attend the court for the determination of the application.

A Dispute Resolution Hearing is not an attended hearing for this purpose.

Most hearings before the Court of Protection will be attended ones, and therefore by virtue of the application of PD 4C, will be heard in public and be subject to a transparency order unless the court has determined that the ordinary position should not apply.

There is scope, under paragraph 2.4 of PD 4C, for the court not to make an order under paragraph 2.1, i.e. that the hearing will be public but subject to a transparency order, and to instead consider whether it should make an order under Rule 4.3(1)(b) (that only part of the hearing should be in public) or Rule 4.3(1)(c) (excluding a person or class of persons from attending a public hearing or part of it).

The matters which the court will consider when deciding whether there is good reason not to make an order for the hearing to be in public and subject to a transparency order, and whether to make an order under Rule 4.3(1) (b) or (c) instead, are set out at paragraph 2.5 of PD 4C. This is set out in full below:

> *2.5. (1) In deciding whether there is good reason not to make an order pursuant to paragraph 2.1 and whether to make an order pursuant to paragraph 2.4 instead, the court will have regard in particular to—*
>
> *(a) the need to protect P or another person involved in the proceedings;*
>
> *(b) the nature of the evidence in the proceedings;*
>
> *(c) whether earlier hearings in the proceedings have taken place in private;*
>
> *(d) whether the court location where the hearing will be held has facilities appropriate to allowing general public access to the hearing, and whether it would be*

practicable or proportionate to move to another location or hearing room;

(e) whether there is any risk of disruption to the hearing if there is general public access to it;

(f) whether, if there is good reason for not allowing general public access, there also exists good reason to deny access to duly accredited representatives of news gathering and reporting organisations.

PD 4C provides that an order pursuant to paragraph 2.1 will ordinarily be in the terms of the standard order approved by the President of the Court of Protection and published on the judicial website.

The link from PD 4C does not currently take you to the precedent order. The court staff should have the template as this is usually issued at the outset of proceedings, when initial case management orders are made on an application.

The Senior Judge, Her Honour Judge Hilder, has recently confirmed[8] that the Rules Committee is currently reviewing the wording of the standard template transparency order, and so it may be that a new template will be published in due course.

The standard terms of the transparency order include an injunction prohibiting the publication of the information which the court has directed cannot be reported or disclosed.

Per Her Honour Judge Hilder in the decision in *VS*: https://www.bailii.org/ew/cases/EWCOP/2024/6.html

Therefore, the transparency order must include a penal notice on the face of the order to make clear that a breach of the order would be contempt of court.

For any public hearing where there is in attendance someone who is not a party to the proceedings, P, or their legal adviser, they should be provided with a copy of the transparency order and asked to confirm that they have read and understood its terms. Ideally this should be done prior to the commencement of the hearing.

Practice Direction 4A

If an application is made for an order under Rules 4.1 to 4.3, where PD 4C does not apply, then this will be governed by Practice Direction 4A – Hearings (Including Reporting Restrictions) (PD 4A)[9].

PD 4A also deals with the procedure for applications for orders imposing different or additional restrictions on the publication of information to those imposed by a transparency order under PD 4C, including applications which are founded on P's Convention Rights.

PD 4A provides that any application for a specific order under Rules 4.1 to 4.3 must be made on a form COP9 Application Notice. The court should then consider whether that application should be considered as a discrete issue.

---

[9] https://www.judiciary.uk/wp-content/uploads/2022/09/pd-4a-hearings-reporting-restrictions.pdf

If an application is being made to impose additional or different restrictions to the information that the court has already determined can be reported, then regard must be had to Part 2 of PD 4A.

By virtue of Section 12(1) of the Administration of Justice Act 1960[10], in respect of proceedings brought under the Mental Capacity Act 2005 where the court is sitting in private, the publication of information about those proceedings would be a contempt of court. However, Rule 4.2(1) provides that such information can be communicated if an order has been made under Rule 4.2(2). Rule 4.2(2) gives the court the power to make an order permitting the publication or communication of such information or material relating to the proceedings as the court may specify or an order permitting the publication of the text or a summary of the whole or part of a judgment or order made by the court.

Rule 4.2(3) also allows the communication of information from a private hearing, subject to the provisions of Part 3 of PD 4A. This includes, but is not limited to, for the purpose of allowing a party to obtain support or advice. Further exemptions allowing the communication of information relating to the proceedings are set out at Part 3 of PD 4A.

Where the court has made an order permitting the publication of information, there is no requirement to give notice that a reporting restrictions order is being made.

The exemption on the requirement to give notice does not apply where the court has already made an order permitting the publication of the information, and therefore where an additional order is sought restricting information that can be reported. In those circumstances, regard must be had to the requirements under section 12(2) of the

10 https://www.legislation.gov.uk/ukpga/Eliz2/8-9/65/contents

Human Rights Act 1998[11] and the applicant seeking to restrict the freedom of expression must have taken all practicable steps to have notified the respondent(s) to that application or must be able to show that there is a compelling reason why notice should not be given.

Notice of an application must also be given in the following circumstances;

I) if a party is inviting the court to impose restrictions or further reporting restrictions based on an application founded on P's convention rights, or the court is considering doing so; or,

II) if the Court has already ordered that proceedings should be in public and an application is being made to vary or increase the reporting restrictions already imposed.

PD 4A provides that this can be effected by serving notice of the application via the Press Association's CopyDirect service.

Whilst the court retains the right to make such orders without notice, PD 4A makes it clear that service should be the norm.

As is noted at paragraph 27 of PD 4A, the aim of any reporting restriction order should be to protect P rather than to confer anonymity on other individuals or organisations, although it is noted that the order may also restrict the identification of others where the absence of such a restriction is likely to prejudice their ability to care for P, or where identification of such persons might lead to identification of P and defeat the purpose of the order. This is explored further in Chapters 3 and 4.

---

11 https://www.legislation.gov.uk/ukpga/1998/42/contents

Paragraph 28 of PD 4A provides that orders will not usually be made prohibiting the publication of material which is already in the public domain, other than in exceptional cases.

At paragraph 29 of PD 4A it is confirmed that such orders should not last for longer than is necessary to achieve the purpose for which they are made.

Any application that is made for further reporting restrictions, or an order made by the court on its own initiative, which invokes P's convention rights will involve a balancing of P's rights under Article 8 (right to respect for private and family life) and the Article 10 (freedom of expression) rights of those who may wish to report information about the proceedings. This is considered in further chapters by reference to the case law in which this balancing exercise has been carried out.

Summary

Following the introduction of PD 4C the position is now that the court will ordinarily make an order that any attended hearing in the Court of Protection shall be in public, but subject to a transparency order which limits the information that can be reported.

This does not however remove the court's power to hold a hearing in private.

The court will need to consider the factors set out at paragraph 2.5 of PD 4C when determining whether the proceedings as a whole or a specific hearing should be heard in private, rather than applying the ordinary approach.

Provision within the Rules also allows the court to make specific orders limiting the information that can be published both in hearings heard in private and those being heard in public.

In the next chapter we will look at specific case examples to consider how the court applies the considerations at paragraph 2.5 when determining whether a matter should be in private or public.

There is scope to interpret quite widely the prohibition on the disclosure of "*any information*" that might lead to the identification of P, a party to the proceedings, or anyone else the court has determined should not be identified.

What is clear from the case law is that there is a tension between the need to protect P and the parties to proceedings, including protecting their privacy, and ensuring that any prohibition on disclosure is proportionate to the infringement on the Article 10 rights of those who may want to report or discuss the facts of the case.

Another issue which has been raised, in the context of transparency orders, is whether the making of a transparency order requires the court to undertake a *Re S* type balancing exercise (see below) as between the Article 8 rights of P and the Article 10 of the public and the press, when making such an order.

As is noted above the introduction of PD 4C has meant that the court will now '*ordinarily*' list a hearing in public and at the same time make an order under Rule 4.3 (i.e. a transparency order) to prohibit the reporting of the information listed in the transparency order.

In his decision in the matter of *Re EM* [2022] EWCOP 31 (29 July 2022)[12], Mr Justice Mostyn expressed some concern about this

12 https://www.bailii.org/ew/cases/EWCOP/2022/31.html

approach, on the basis that such orders will be made routinely and therefore without the carrying out of the *Re S* type balancing exercise required when making an order which restricts what information can be reported/disclosed from proceedings.

Mr Justice Mostyn suggested that the Rules Committee may wish to consider the standard practice of making transparency orders. As noted above, the Rules Committee is reported to be reviewing the standard wording of transparency orders. It is not known whether this will extend to addressing the points made by Mr Justice Mostyn about the making of transparency orders in standard terms, which continues to be the practice.

In the matter of *Hillingdon Hospitals NHS Foundation Trust v IN & Ors* [2023] EWCOP 32 (21 July 2023)[13], Mr Justice Poole considered the matter of the transparency order, confirming that he agreed with the analysis of Mr Justice Mostyn that the transparency order is a form of reporting restrictions order. He noted in the judgment that although the transparency order allows the proceedings to be heard in public, it also restricts what can be reported. As such, applying the authorities, including the decision of the Court of Appeal in *Abbasi v Newcastle Upon Tyne Hospitals NHS Foundation Trust and Ors* [2023] EWCA Civ 331[14] and PD 4C, the conclusion of Mr Justice Poole was that when considering whether to make a transparency order the court must still carry out the balancing exercise described by Lord Steyn in *Re S* [2004] UKHL 47[15]; i.e. balancing the competing Article 8 and Article 10 convention rights. The application of this balancing exercise is considered in the following chapters, by reference to the case law.

13 https://www.bailii.org/ew/cases/EWCOP/2023/32.html

14 https://www.bailii.org/ew/cases/EWCA/Civ/2023/331.html

15 https://www.bailii.org/uk/cases/UKHL/2004/47.html

CHAPTER TWO

PRIVACY

Private hearings and reporting

As confirmed in the previous chapter, the general rule under the Court of Protection Rules is that hearings in the Court of Protection will be held in private but with the court having the power to make an order to authorise a person, or a class of persons, to attend a hearing or a part of the hearing.

The court also has the power to authorise the reporting and sharing of information from the proceedings even if they are being heard in private.

Since the introduction of PD 4C, however, the court will now ordinarily direct that a hearing is to be in public and will within that same order make provisions for the restriction of what information can be reported or shared outside of the proceedings.

Often this will involve the anonymisation of P. In his decision in *Sunderland City Council v Macpherson (Rev1)* [2023] EWCOP 3 (20 January 2023)[16], Mr Justice Poole addressed the question of why it is "*the standard, but not invariable, practice in the Court of Protection, to make orders preventing the identification of P (the protected person)*", giving the following reasons at paragraph 28 of his judgment:

[16] https://www.bailii.org/ew/cases/EWCOP/2023/3.html

"i *The proceedings will often involve matters which would ordinarily be regarded as of a confidential nature involving the private life of P, including their health.*

ii. *The proceedings are usually brought by a public body such as a Local Authority or an NHS Trust – P has not chosen to become involved in litigation.*

iii. *P will often not have the mental capacity to give their informed consent to details about their private lives.*

iv. *The invasion of privacy caused by identifying P, and P's awareness that others know information about their private lives, would not only be a breach of their Convention rights, but can often be harmful to P's mental state or their welfare."*

Notwithstanding the ordinary approach introduced by PD 4C, there may be cases where the court considers that reporting restrictions and anonymisation are not sufficient and that there are grounds for the proceedings to remain in private.

In those cases, the court will then need to consider whether it should allow any attendance by identified persons, for example by accredited members of the press. There may be occasions when, due to the issues involved or the need to protect P, the balance falls in favour of proceedings remaining completely private.

In addition to allowing attendance at a private hearing or authorising the reporting or sharing of information from proceedings that are in private, the court also has the option of publishing its judgment from a case heard in private.

The balancing exercise: Article 8 ECHR v Article 10 ECHR

In deciding whether to make some aspects of the court's decision-making public, for example by allowing limited reporting of the proceedings, or by allowing the attendance of accredited members of the press to attend hearings, or by publishing a judgment, the court will need to carry out a balancing exercise of the Article 8 rights of P as against the Article 10 rights of the wider public.

This balancing exercise is set out by Lord Steyn in paragraph 17 of the judgment in *Re S (a child)* [2004] UKHL 47[17], as follows:

> "*The interplay between articles 8 and 10 has been illuminated by the opinions in the House of Lords in Campbell v MGN Ltd [2004] 2 WLR 1232. For present purposes the decision of the House on the facts of Campbell and the differences between the majority and the minority are not material. What does, however, emerge clearly from the opinions are four propositions. First, neither article has as such precedence over the other. Secondly, where the values under the two articles are in conflict, an intense focus on the comparative importance of the specific rights being claimed in the individual case is necessary. Thirdly, the justifications for interfering with or restricting each right must be taken into account. Finally, the proportionality test must be applied to each. For convenience I will call this the ultimate balancing test.*"

Article 10 of the European Convention on Human Rights (ECHR) provides:

17 https://www.bailii.org/uk/cases/UKHL/2004/47.html

Article 10 – Freedom of Expression

1. Everyone has the right to freedom of expression. This right shall include freedom to hold opinions and to receive and impart information and ideas without interference by public authority and regardless of frontiers. This Article shall not prevent States from requiring the licensing of broadcasting, television or cinema enterprises.

2. The exercise of these freedoms, since it carries with it duties and responsibilities, may be subject to such formalities, conditions, restrictions or penalties as are prescribed by law and are necessary in a democratic society, in the interests of national security, territorial integrity or public safety, for the prevention of disorder or crime, for the protection of health or morals, for the protection of the reputation or rights of others, for preventing the disclosure of information received in confidence, or for maintaining the authority and impartiality of the judiciary.

Article 8 of the ECHR provides:

Article 8 – Right to respect for private and family life

1. Everyone has the right to respect for his private and family life, his home, and his correspondence.

2. There shall be no interference by a public authority with the exercise of this right except such as is in accordance with the law and is necessary in a democratic society in the interests of national security, public safety or the economic wellbeing of the country, for the prevention of disorder or crime, for the protection of health or morals, or for the protection of the rights and freedoms of others.

Neither Article 10.1 or Article 8.1 are absolute, and both may be subject to interference as set out in Articles 10.2 and 8.2 respectively.

In determining the issue of whether to hold a Court of Protection hearing in private or public, and in considering whether and to what extent to allow reporting of the information from those proceedings, the Court of Protection is carrying out the "ultimate balancing test" described by Lord Steyn in *Re S*, applying these competing rights.

Key to this exercise is the level of interference with the respective convention rights, and the proportionality of that interference having regard to the specific facts of the case.

In an earlier decision of the Court of Protection which preceded the introduction of PD 4C, *W v M & Ors* [2011] EWCOP 1197 (12 May 2011)[18], the court observed that "*when focusing on the article 8 rights of P and any other relevant person, the court should consider the nature and strength of the evidence of the risk of harm. There must, as Peter Jackson J observed in Hillingdon LBC v Neary [2011] EWHC 413 (COP) at paragraph 15(3), be a proper, factual basis for such concerns*". [paragraph 40].

In the same decision, in considering the important public interest arguments for the practice and procedure of the Court of Protection to be more widely understood, reference was made to the following quote from the decision in *Hillingdon LBC v Neary* [2011] EWHC 413 (COP)[19];

> *"There is a genuine public interest in the work of this court being understood. Not only is this healthy in itself – the presence of the media in appropriate cases has a bracing effect*

18 https://www.bailii.org/ew/cases/EWCOP/2011/1197.html

19 https://www.bailii.org/ew/cases/EWCOP/2011/1377.html

> *on all public servants, whether in the field of social services or the law – but it may also help to dispel misunderstandings. It is not in the interests of individual litigants, or of society at large, for a court that is by definition devoted to the protection of the welfare of disadvantaged people to be characterised (including in a report about this case, published as I write this judgment) as 'secretive'. It is part of our natural curiosity to want to know other people's secrets, and using pejorative descriptions of this kind may stimulate interest. The opportunity, in appropriate cases, to follow a process that has welfare, not secrecy, at its heart can only help the media to produce balanced reporting, and not fall back on clichés."*

The case law

This balancing exercise was considered in the context of Court of Protection proceedings in the matter of *A Local Authority v H* [2023] EWCOP 4 (07 February 2023)[20].

This matter concerned H, a young adult and a natal male who now identified as female. H had experienced considerable trauma and abuse in her childhood. H experienced complex psychological and psychiatric challenges: global developmental delay; attention deficit hyperactivity disorder; executive dysfunction; developmental trauma disorder; and possibly emotionally unstable personality disorder as a result of her traumatic and abusive childhood.

H had expressed an interest in pre-pubescent children and this was said to almost certainly arise as a consequence of the abuse she had suffered. A psychiatrist instructed in the proceedings identified H as presenting a real risk of sexual harm to children. H was subject to a

20 https://www.bailii.org/ew/cases/EWCOP/2023/4.html

very restrictive care regime, under which she was said to have progressed strikingly well. The court was dealing with a determination of H's capacity to make decisions in a number of domains.

Mr Justice Hayden, dealing with this case, noted the importance of public scrutiny of the difficult decisions the Court of Protection is asked to take. However, he also noted that "*Occasionally, however, the compelling arguments for transparency are required to yield to the equally compelling need to protect the most vulnerable*" [paragraph 31].

In considering the competing rights Mr Justice Hayden noted, at paragraph 33 of his judgment, that a balance has to be struck on the facts of each individual case, having regard to the relevant competing interests in focus i.e. the Article 8 rights of P and the Article 10 rights of the public at large, as exercised by those wanting to report on the proceedings.

In assessing the balance between Article 8 and Article 10, Mr Justice Hayden noted that the test as set out by Lord Steyn in *Re S* makes it clear that neither of these rights "*is afforded greater weight*", and that "*Where a restriction on either right is contemplated, the <u>proportionality</u> of that restriction falls to be considered in what Lord Steyn calls "the ultimate balancing test"*." [paragraph 34, own emphasis added].

In considering the factors relevant to his decision, Mr Justice Hayden noted the vulnerability of H, and the importance of constructing "*a carapace of privacy*" to protect H at "*this most important time in her life*".

The judge noted that the background facts would likely generate public interest and also that the particular sensitivity of "*that of the natal male, who self-identifies as female but who has not embarked upon treatment for the purpose of modifying her sexual characteristics.*" [paragraph 35], and the fact that H presents a sexual risk to children.

Leading the judge to opine that "*It is not difficult to imagine that not only H's privacy but her safety might be compromised were her identity to be in the public domain.*" [paragraph 35].

The analysis therefore fell "*decidedly*" in favour of H's Article 8 rights. The judge therefore continued to hear the matter in private but gave permission for legal bloggers and accredited journalists to remain in the hearing, and in addition allowed no reporting during the hearing.

That the judgment was published recognised the "*legitimate public interest*" in the highly sensitive issues in the case. The judge made it clear that he had endeavoured to put those issues in the public domain, in a way which would protect H's identity.

At paragraph 32 of the judgment, the judge also noted the importance of identifying the applicable legal framework, noting that the well-established principle of open justice was articulated by Mr Justice Toulson in the decision of *Guardian News and Media Ltd, R (on the application of) v City of Westminster Magistrates Court* [2012] EWCA Civ 420[21], as referenced in the introduction to this guide.

What can be seen from this case is that the court recognises the importance of the principle of open justice, but that careful consideration must be given to the facts of the individual case when considering whether to lift the restrictions on reporting or sharing information about what are often deeply personal and sensitive decisions being made by the court, and to what extent.

21 Guardian News and Media Ltd, R (on the application of) v City of Westminster Magistrates' Court [2012] EWCA Civ 420 (03 April 2012) (bailii.org)

Another case which considered the issue of whether proceedings should be heard in private was that of *Re P* [2019] EWCOP 42 (01 October 2019)[22], in which the facts were quite stark.

The case concerned an application for authority to execute a Statutory Will on behalf of P, and the applicant wanted to withhold service of the application from P's son, who was referred to in the published judgment as X.

X's behaviour was described as "*extreme*" and the court was given evidence of a number of violent incidents from X, and also threats to harm and kill members of his family. He was subject to a restraining order and had just recently served a prison sentence for breaching the restraining order.

It was noted in the judgment that "*X presently has no idea of the value of his father's estate; and if he were to learn of it because of these proceedings, his menacing behaviour – which has often been focused on obtaining money – would be aggravated, leading to very real risks to the safety of others and potentially jeopardising P's care home placement*" [paragraph 37].

It was argued that the risk of X finding out about proceedings from any reporting of the proceedings would undermine a decision not to notify X of the application.

The court determined that the matter should continue being heard in private but that an anonymised judgment would be published confirming the decision not to notify X of the application and giving the reasons for this decision.

22 https://www.bailii.org/ew/cases/EWCOP/2019/42.html

The judge noted; "'*In those circumstances, even though the evidence of matters on which their fears are based is untested, I am satisfied that there is need for the court to take an approach which protects P, the Applicants and members of the wider family from the kind of behaviour which has led to imprisonment for breach of a restraining order. The (very real) public interest in open justice can be met by an order permitting publication of this judgment, and future consideration of such an order in relation to any judgment on the substantive application*". [Paragraph 40].

Further consideration was given to the issue of proceedings remaining in private in the matter of *Kent County Council v P & Anor* [2022] EWCOP 3 (04 February 2022)[23], which is looked at further in Chapter 3.

These were proceedings which had initially been heard in private and, until that hearing, the judge had concluded should remain in private. Arguments were made which included that the information which concerned the court was extremely private and "*at the more prurient end of the scale*", and that therefore the potential infringement of P's Article 8 rights was significant, justifying the matter remaining in private.

In concluding that the time had come to allow the matter to be heard in public, with reporting restrictions, the judge noted that there is an important public interest in holding court hearings in public and allowing the press to report on them, and that therefore the presumption should be for open hearings unless there are strong countervailing factors for doing so. The infringement of P's Article 8 rights was not considered significant enough to keep the proceedings private. This decision is considered in more depth in the next chapter.

[23] https://www.bailii.org/ew/cases/EWCOP/2022/3.html

In the matter of *Re G (Adult) [2014]* EWCOP 1361 (01 May 2014)[24], which predated the introduction of PD 4C, the court had to grapple with an application by Associated News Limited to be joined as a party to the proceedings, in support of its applications to be able to report on the matter.

An issue which the court also considered, albeit acknowledging that there was in fact no such application before it, was the question of whether the Article 8 rights of those wanting to report were also engaged.

In considering specifically the role of the press, the court noted "*the State has a positive obligation under Article 8 to ensure that X's right to respect for private life is not violated as a result of press intrusion or harassment: see, for example, Von Hannover v Germany (2003) 40 EHRR 1, [2004] EMLR 379, para 57, and Rekos v Greece [2009] EMLR 290, paras 35, 41*". [Paragraph 23].

In considering the particular question of whether the Article 8 rights of those wishing to report on the matter are engaged, the court noted, at paragraphs 24 and 25 of the judgment:

> "*Secondly, if for whatever reason, good or bad, reasonable or unreasonable, or if indeed for no reason at all, X does not wish to have anything to do with Y, then Y cannot impose himself on X by praying in aid his own Article 8 rights. For X can pray in aid, against Y, X's own Article 8 right to decide who is to be excluded from X's 'inner circle', and in that contest, if X is a competent adult, X's Article 8 rights must trump Y's. It necessarily follows from this that, absent any issue as to X's*

24 https://www.bailii.org/ew/cases/EWCOP/2014/1361.html

> *capacity or undue influence, X's refusal to associate with Y cannot give rise to any justiciable issue as between Y and X.*
>
> *Thirdly, if X lacks capacity, Y's Article 8 rights can no more trump X's rights than if X had capacity. Y cannot impose himself on X by praying in aid his own Article 8 rights. Y's Article 8 rights have to be weighed and assessed in the balance against X's Article 8 rights. If Y's rights and X's rights conflict, then both domestic law and the Strasbourg jurisprudence require the conflict to be resolved by reference to X's best interests. X's best interests are determinative. As I said in Re S, para 45, referring to what Sedley LJ had said in In re F (Adult: Court's Jurisdiction) [2001] Fam 38, 57:*
>
>> *"In the final analysis, as Sedley LJ put the point, it is the mentally incapacitated adult's welfare which must remain throughout the single issue (emphasis added). The court's concern must be with his safety and welfare."*

It is clear from the above case law that it is the welfare and safety of P which the court will be focused on, albeit that this will need to be balanced against any competing Article 10 rights and the important principle of open justice.

Summary

What can be seen from the case of *A Local Authority v H*, above, is that the court will seek to strike a balance between protecting the rights of P and ensuring that the important need for transparency and openness are being met in the decisions being taken by the Court of Protection.

As the judge noted, the facts in H's case were particularly sensitive and likely to concern the wider public, who would want to understand how the court was reaching decisions about H's residence and care.

The court was acutely aware of the importance of the principles of open justice and the importance of allowing the wider public to understand the rationale behind the decisions being taken by the Court of Protection.

In using its powers to restrict both the scope of those able to attend the hearing and therefore report on it, and also the timing of that reporting, the court was able to balance the need to protect P's rights and also ensure that the Article 10 rights of the wider public were given effect.

In the matter of *Re P* the court was grappling with the difficult issue of ensuring that it could give effect to its decision not to notify X of the application, but at the same time provide an explanation of the basis for such a decision given that it would inevitably interfere with X's Article 6 rights. No doubt the wider public would want to understand how such a decision was reached and how the court justified this in balancing the rights of X and those members of the family who had been subject to threats from X.

The publication of an anonymised judgment enabled the court's decision making to be transparent and shared with the wider public, whilst still ensuring that the proceedings could remain effective and that the application to withhold notification of the proceedings on X would not be frustrated.

The importance of the principle of open justice is clear and recognised by the court. In the decision of *Davies v Wigan Council & Anor* [2020] EWCOP 60 (23 November 2020)[25], the following passage of Lady Hale's judgment in *Re (C) v the Secretary of State for Justice* [2016] UKSC 2 was noted:

---

25 https://www.bailii.org/ew/cases/EWCOP/2020/60.html

> "*The principle of open justice is one of the most precious in our law. It is there to reassure the public and the parties that our courts are indeed doing justice according to law. In fact, there are two aspects to this principle. The first is that justice should be done in open court, so that the people interested in the case, the wider public and the media can know what is going on. The court should not hear and take into account evidence and arguments that they have not heard or seen. The second is that the names of the people whose cases are being decided, and others involved in the hearing, should be public knowledge. The rationale for the second rule is not quite the same as the rationale for the first, as we shall see...*"

As is seen from the decisions considered in this guide, there are of courses cases where the balance falls in favour of the Article 8 rights and in keeping the matter private or limiting the reporting of information from proceedings, however it is clear that there is a strong presumption of open justice within the Court of Protection which has been further developed by the introduction of PD 4C. The next two chapters consider in more detail the case law relating to the application of the Practice Direction and the use of transparency orders.

CHAPTER THREE

TRANSPARENCY

It is helpful to look at the case law decided since the introduction of PD 4C, to understand how the Court of Protection has approached the use of transparency orders.

Transparency Orders – P's information

One of the earliest reported cases considering the use of transparency orders was *Re P (Court of Protection: Transparency)* [2019] EWCOP 67 (11 November 2019)[26]

The facts of the case were that the subject of the proceedings, P, was a 25-year-old young man with a diagnosis of a mild learning disability combined with significant deficits in adaptive functioning.

He had autistic spectrum disorder (ASD) and attention deficit hyperactivity disorder (ADHD). His cognitive impairment and concomitant ASD and ADHD placed him at risk of offending and at the time of the judgment he had been convicted of several sexual offences.

He was subject to a Sexual Harm Prevention Order and to an extant suspended sentence of four months' imprisonment suspended for twelve months, with part of the sentence being a requirement that he reside at a particular placement.

---

26 https://www.bailii.org/ew/cases/EWCOP/2019/67.html

The case had commenced in private when before another judge, however when it came before Mr Justice Keehan he raised the question of whether the matter should now be heard in public but subject to a transparency order.

As explained in the judgment, prior to the introduction of PD 4C there had been accusations in the media of the Court of Protection operating as a 'secret court'[27], following cases that had garnered press interest, but which had then been heard in private and were therefore unable to be reported on. The court noted that there was also a concern that there could be cases about which the press and wider public were unaware, such that they would also not be aware that there were issues in which the public might have an interest.

Mr Justice Keehan noted at paragraph 7 of his judgment, that "*The background to the "usual approach" was a desire to ensure that the Court of Protection, which has the power to make a wide range of orders involving those who lack capacity including medical treatment and deprivation of liberty orders, avoided the label of "the secret court". This label had been adopted by numerous press organisations. The concept of a "secret court" had the potential to undermine the confidence of the important work of the Court of Protection*".

Mr Justice Keehan acknowledged the importance of considering the need to safeguard the person who was the subject of the proceedings, noting that "*When considering the factors set out in PD 4C, the need to protect P is a very powerful factor in favour of holding the proceedings in private.*"

---

27 Some examples: https://www.dailymail.co.uk/news/article-1222764/Secret-court-seizes-3-2bn-elderly-mentally-impaired.html and https://www.telegraph.co.uk/news/2016/10/16/the-terrifying-tale-of-how-britains-most-secret-court-imprisoned/

He also acknowledged, however, that this must be balanced against the need for transparency and open justice. At paragraph 16 of the judgment, he noted "*The importance of public justice, however, is a central tenet of the Court of Protection. It should only be overridden when the circumstances of the case compellingly, and on the basis of cogent evidence, require the proceedings to be heard in private.*"

To reach a decision that allowed the proceedings to be reported on whilst still protecting P, the judge balanced the factors at PD 4C and excluded members of the public but allowed in accredited press and made a transparency order setting out what information the press could not report. The decision does not set out the terms of the transparency order made.

Another case which considered the balancing of the factors in PD 4C was the case of *Kent County Council v P & Anor* [2022] EWCOP 3 (04 February 2022)[28].

Mrs Justice Lieven noted in that case that when deciding if there is good reason to depart from the 'ordinary rule' of making an order under PD 4C, the court will consider the matters set out in paragraph 2.5 of PD 4C as well as the fact that the court can protect participants and the integrity of proceedings by making a transparency order which limits the information that can be reported and disclosed outside of the proceedings, rather than keeping proceedings private.

The facts of that case were that P, who was 21 years old at the time of the judgment, had been recovered from her parents' home in late Summer 2019 after concerns had been raised by her paternal aunt and grandmother. She was found by police in a state of extreme neglect, suffering from malnutrition and in an exceptionally poor state of care.

---

28 https://www.bailii.org/ew/cases/EWCOP/2022/3.html

Following her removal, P was looked after in her own property with support from professional carers and NHS bodies. She had suffered physically and mentally as a result of her traumatic experiences.

When the case first came before Mrs Justice Lieven in September 2020, she shared the parties' concerns about the great sensitivity of the case and the potential press interest given the manner in which P was found.

However, at a hearing in October 2021, Mrs Justice Lieven expressed concerns about the length of time being taken by the police to conclude their investigation and reach a charging decision against P's parents, the investigation being part of the reason why the proceedings had continued to be heard in private up until that hearing. Mrs Justice Lieven agreed to keep the matter private until the next review, which was listed on 18 November 2021.

As can be seen from the judgment and the submissions made on behalf of P, there was a concern on P's behalf that the information before the court in this case was "*deeply personal*" and at the "*more prurient end of the scale*" and so may attract particular media interest which could then impact on P.

The local authority also noted "*the risk that P would be able to be identified relatively easily because of the almost unique nature of the case and the initial press coverage relating to it*". The local authority also noted that there was evidence that P "*becomes upset if she thinks people are talking about her and that she appears to be concerned about her privacy*".

It is clear from the submissions that a concern about protecting the person who was the subject of the proceedings formed the basis of the arguments being made by the parties against the opening up of the proceedings.

The local authority argued that although there may be a legitimate public interest in the police and criminal justice process, there was no similar legitimate public interest in the Court of Protection proceedings and the "*very personal and intimate information which is necessarily before the Court of Protection*".

A separate argument made by Kent Police was their concern about the potential impact on the integrity of a future criminal trial if proceedings were heard in public and the press were allowed to report on it. This may well be a relevant consideration for other proceedings where there are outstanding criminal charges against a party or which relate to P where, for example, P is the victim of a crime.

Consideration should be given in those cases to whether the disclosure of information into the public domain, via the Court of Protection proceedings, could prejudice any criminal proceedings that have been, or may be, brought. As can be seen from the judgment, in this case this was not considered a strong argument against a hearing being held in public. Therefore, the existence of parallel criminal proceedings involving P is not an automatic factor which will cause the court to apply the general rule of holding the hearing(s) in private.

In this case, Mrs Justice Lieven concluded that there is an important public interest in holding court hearings in public and allowing the press to report on them, and that therefore the presumption should be for open hearings unless there are strong countervailing factors for doing so.

The two countervailing factors she identified were interference with P's privacy and her Article 8 rights, and a potential impact on a criminal trial.

In terms of the impact on P's Article 8 rights the judge noted that initially she agreed the proceedings should remain private given the unusual facts and consequent danger of P being identified and being distressed by her personal information being in the public domain; however as time had gone on and P had not engaged with the outside world as much as it had been hoped she might, the risk to her of hearing or seeing something being reported and connecting it to herself was now considered "*quite remote*". The risk of personal distress to her was therefore "*significantly less*" than initially feared. The interference with P's Article 8 rights was therefore "*a limited one*".

This has to be balanced against the Article 10 rights and the public's legitimate interest in knowing what has happened in proceedings. The judged noted at paragraph 29 of the judgment that "*There is a legitimate public interest in the fact that deeply distressing cases, such as that of P, happen in the UK and how they are dealt with by the relevant authorities*". The police investigation had taken two and a half years and had still not reached a charging decision, and the judge noted that delays in the system of justice were a matter of legitimate public interest.

The judge dismissed the arguments of Kent Police that reporting on the Court of Protection proceedings might undermine the integrity of the criminal trial, noting firstly that the nature of the evidence in the Court of Protection is about P's welfare and not the conduct, and culpability, of her parents. The judge also noted that it is often the case that there are civil proceedings or inquiries in the public domain before a future criminal trial, citing the Grenfell Tower inquiry and Manchester Arena inquiry as examples.

The balance as between P's Article 8 rights and the Article 10 rights of the press, and the public interest, therefore came down in favour of allowing reporting with a transparency order to protect P's identity.

Transparency orders – information of other parties/individuals

Transparency orders are not just used to prohibit the identification of P, or their family members. These orders are routinely used to also protect the identity of clinicians or professionals involved in the care of P albeit that this is generally on the basis that such restrictions will ensure that P's care is not affected.

There have been a number of recently reported cases in which the Court has made a transparency order in cases involving serious medical treatment decisions, to include prohibiting the identity of the clinicians involved in treating P, noting in doing so that there was no, or very limited, public interest in naming those clinicians and noting the importance in those clinicians being able to carry out their clinical functions and care for P.Decisions in the matters of *H, Re (An Adult; Termination)* [2023] EWCOP 183 (24 October 2023)[29], *Manchester University NHS Foundation Trust v Mr Y & Ors* [2023] EWCOP 51 (15 November 2023)[30] and *University Hospitals Southampton NHS Foundation Trust v Miss T & Ors* [2023] EWCOP 54 (17 November 2023)[31] all included such an order.

The Court has recently grappled with the issue of the routine practice by which indefinite anonymity orders applied to medical and non-medical carers were being made in end of life cases. In the case of*Abbasi & Anor v Newcastle Upon Tyne Hospitals NHS Foundation Trust* [2023] EWCA Civ 331[32], a decision of the Court of Appeal in respect of cases being heard in the High Court under the inherent

29 https://www.bailii.org/ew/cases/EWCOP/2023/183.html

30 https://www.bailii.org/ew/cases/EWCOP/2023/51.html

31 https://www.bailii.org/ew/cases/EWCOP/2023/54.html

32 https://www.bailii.org/ew/cases/EWCA/Civ/2023/331.html

jurisdiction, the Court of Appeal quite strongly concluded that this being done as a routine practice could not be justified.

The issue of anonymity orders being granted in respect of treating clinicians and health and care professionals engaged with P in proceeding in the Court of Protection was again considered in the decision in *University Hospitals Birmingham NHS Foundation Trust v Thirumalesh & Ors* [2023] EWCOP 43 (29 September 2023)[33].

Following serious medical treatment proceedings in the Court of Protection concerning ST, who is named in the judgment, an application was made by ST's parents to lift the transparency order which had been made at an earlier in the proceedings.

At the point at which that application was heard, ST had sadly died.

Noting that the application to discharge the transparency order had been made earlier in the proceedings, but that the transparency order was continued by consent, Mr Justice Peel observed "*I have little doubt that the courts (myself included), when faced with complex and wide-ranging issues about capacity and best interests at hearings with limited court time, followed the usual practice of continuing the anonymisation at least until conclusion of the proceedings at which point fuller consideration could be given to the issue.*" [Paragraph 7].

As is noted in the judgment it had already been agreed that the restrictions on identifying ST, her family and any expert witnesses should be lifted immediately.

The dispute that was before the court therefore was whether the restrictions on identifying the Trust, the hospital at which ST was treated and clinical/nursing staff should be lifted. ST's family sought

33 https://www.bailii.org/ew/cases/EWCOP/2023/43.html

the immediate discharge of those restrictions and the Trust sought to have the restrictions continue for a period of eight weeks after which they would be discharged automatically.

Referring to the decision of the Court of Appeal in the *Abbasi* case referred to above, Mr Justice Peel noted that the Court of Appeal had acknowledged "*that a short term RRO preserving anonymity to protect the integrity of the proceedings may be justified*" [paragraph 30.i] and that the issue which the Court of Appeal was primarily concerned with was the continuation of those orders beyond the end of the proceedings.

Other relevant points noted from the Court of Appeal decision in *Abbasi* were set out in paragraph 30 of the judgment;

> "*vii) In weighing the competing Article 8 and Article 10 considerations, a generic class of anonymisation for swathes of professionals engaged in this work, based on systemic concerns about general morale, recruitment and well-being of health staff, but which is divorced from the individual circumstances of a particular case, is not appropriate (paras 116 to 129 generally).*
>
> *viii) "Conferring lifelong anonymity through indefinite orders irrespective of the individual circumstances of those protected...is something which the courts should do only in "the most compelling of circumstances"" (para 119).*
>
> *ix) Each individual case requires "careful scrutiny, clear evidence and an intense evaluation of competing interests" before continuing an anonymity order beyond the end of the proceedings (para 121).*
>
> *x) "Where the publication concerns a question "of general interest", article 10(2) scarcely leaves any room for*

> *restriction on freedom of expression" (para 123) and, having considered the meaning of general public interest, "The issues arising from end-of-life cases fall into this broad category (para 124)".*

It was noted that the decision in *Abbasi* is the subject of an appeal to the Supreme Court, and so there may be further determinations made by the Supreme Court on the points above.

In deciding to immediately lift the restrictions on identifying ST, Mr Justice Peel noted that there was now no justification in not naming her and the balance between the Article 8 and Article 10 rights fell decidedly in favour of naming her. This was also determined to be the case in respect of ST's family.

In deciding to leave in place the restrictions on identifying any members of the clinical or treating staff for eight weeks, Mr Justice Peel noted "*In respect of the identification of clinicians, the family allege failings on the part of certain individuals, stating in terms that this amounted to negligence which led to the death of ST. Although the family, I accept, have no intention to take any steps which might lead to harassment of named staff, the harsh reality of modern methods of communications, particularly by social media, is that they will have no control over the narrative. The publicity generated by this case has been heated in some quarters. There is likely to be heightened interest in the coming days as a result of my intention that the restrictions on identifying ST and her family should be immediately lifted. If anonymisation of clinicians is lifted, the consequences are unpredictable, but there is in my judgment a risk that abuse and harassment may follow, particularly as they may be reported by the family as having given ST inadequate care. Were that to come to pass, I would regard it as a very considerable interference with their Article 8 rights. That risk is likely to be at its most acute in the next few weeks and I consider that there should be a "cooling off period" measured in weeks. That would be a proportionate interference with the family's and the media's Article 10 rights, given the potential interference with the clinical/nursing staff Article 8 rights."* [Paragraph 43].

Mr Justice Peel lifted the restrictions on reporting the name of the Trust that was treating ST, however retained the restriction on identifying the hospital at which ST was treated in light of concerns about the risk of jigsaw identification of staff.

Summary

The judgments in *Re P (Court of Protection: Transparency)* and *Kent County Council v P & Anor* highlight the Court of Protection's commitment to the important principle of open justice and the need for transparency within its decision making.

Whilst the need to protect P was considered in both cases to be a strong factor weighing against the opening up of the proceedings, the ability to protect P through the use of a transparency order ultimately allowed the court to ensure transparency of the proceedings whilst still protecting P.

In the matter of *Kent County Council v P & Anor*, consideration was given to the impact on P if she were able to identify herself as the subject of the reporting. It was noted that this was initially a concern of the judge but that P's greater connection with the outside world had, unfortunately, not materialised, such that this issue was considered less likely to arise. It is not clear whether the balance would have tipped against the proceedings being heard in public, and being able to be reported on, if P had for example been more engaged with the outside world and therefore there had been a greater risk of identifying herself from any reporting of the case and consequently becoming distressed. It may be that in those circumstances the court would have been inclined to keep the matter in private.

This is an interesting consideration as one can imagine that there will be individuals who are the subject of Court of Protection proceedings, often brought not at their instigation, who may object to the wider world knowing about their affairs.

Additionally, there are likely to be individuals who may find themselves the subject of proceedings in the Court of Protection who are engaged with technology and media, including social media, and who may therefore be exposed to reporting and commentary on their cases.

It is not considered in the judgment, given the fact that the risk of P being more connected with the outside world was low, however it is an interesting question as to what level of harm would be required to tip the balance in favour of keeping proceedings private and/or preventing the reporting of information from the proceedings. This is an issue which has to date remained very fact specific in the judgments dealing with an argument that transparency or reporting might cause harm to P, and it may be that it is not possible for the court to be prescriptive on this point.

In the decision in *ST*, summarising the Court of Appeal's reasoning, Mr Justice Peel identified the following points that may be relevant to this consideration, at paragraph 30 of his judgment;

> *"ii) Although there is no hierarchical primacy between Articles 8 and 10, "....the practical realities of the balance in such cases will be that evidence of a compelling nature is needed to curtail the legitimate exercise of free speech" (para 78).*

> *iii) In so far as article 8 is engaged on one side of the balance there must be a careful analysis of the risk (para 88). The threshold required to be met is that "the publication in question had constituted such a serious interference with his private life as to undermine his personal integrity"."*

Although the court in *Kent County Council v P & Anor* was not persuaded by the arguments of Kent Police that reporting would potentially impact on any future criminal trial, I suggest that it is still worth considering this. If there is a live criminal investigation or safeguarding investigation connected with a case, consideration should be given to whether this might be impacted by any reporting or wider discussion of the proceedings, such that consideration should be given to whether the proceedings should remain private or whether specific or greater restrictions on reporting should be imposed. It may be that this is only required until the conclusion of such an investigation, although as noted in the judgment in *Kenty County Council v P & Anor*, the length of time that the investigation was taking was one of the matters which the court considered was in the public interest to be reported.

CHAPTER FOUR

LIFTING REPORTING RESTRICTIONS

The previous chapters have discussed the operation of the Rules and Practice Direction 4C, in terms of the use of transparency orders, and the use of reporting restrictions orders under Rule 4.2, to permit reporting of cases in the Court of Protection, whilst still protecting the privacy of P and others involved in the proceedings by restricting the information which could be reported so as to protect their anonymity.

There are, however, occasions when the court has disapplied parts of the transparency order or reporting restrictions order, in order to allow the reporting of the identity of P.

Different considerations have applied when making such a decision and it is therefore worthwhile considering the reported cases in which this has happened, to examine the reasons for the court's decision in each one.

Lifting the restrictions

One such case is *PH & Anor v Brighton And Hove City Council* [2021] EWCOP 63 (23 November 2021)[34].

34 https://www.bailii.org/ew/cases/EWCOP/2021/63.html

This judgment deals specifically with two applications by the press in welfare proceedings in the Court of Protection, with the substantive matters being dealt with separately.

The case is that of Tony Hickmott who at the time of the judgment had been detained for almost two decades. There had been previous reporting of Mr Hickmott's situation in national media and an earlier published judgment in the Administrative Court in judicial review proceedings brought on Mr Hickmott's behalf, which gave extensive detail of Mr Hickmott's characteristics and circumstances.

The applicants in the Court of Protection proceedings had therefore raised a concern that because of the information already in the public domain, the effect of the transparency order was to effectively prevent any reporting of those proceedings because of the risk of jigsaw identification of Mr Hickmott from the information already made public.

In paragraph 11 of her judgment, Her Honour Judge Hilder noted that the standard approach of hearings being public but subject to a transparency order, in accordance with the Rules and PD 4C, "*is intended by the Court of Protection to reconcile the personal nature of information which is likely to be disclosed in Court of Protection proceedings, and the public's need to understand and have confidence in the Court's decision-making process*"

She confirmed that the anonymity provided for in the transparency order can be relaxed, and the test for relaxation is "*the "familiar" balancing test between Articles 8 and 10 of the European Convention on Human Rights.Article 8, of course, protects privacy and family life; Article 10 protects freedom of expression.And the classic exposition of the balancing exercise is that of Lord Steyn in Re S (A Child) (Identification: Restrictions on Publication) 2005 1 AC 593 at [17]*" [paragraph 12]. This test is set out in chapter 2.

The factors that the judge considered weighed in favour of lifting the reporting restrictions were set out at paragraph 29 of the judgment:

- Proper public interest – "*A man has been detained for many years beyond the point when clinicians considered him fit for discharge.Resource pressures are at least a part of that story, there being nowhere else to meet his needs.I have no doubt that this is an issue on which there should be open public debate on an informed basis.*";

- Tony Hickmott's parents supported reporting and were unable to share their story and their struggles to restore their family life without the restrictions being lifted;

- A lot of information was already in the public domain, and the particular facts of the case would make it very easy to identify Mr Hickmott with "*limited skills of Google searching*". The judge considered the contention that any reporting was effectively prohibited by the risk of jigsaw identification of "*significant weight*". Expressing concern "*that where the facts of this matter are much known about in advance, and are likely to be known about if and when proceedings come to an end, that the maintaining of the Transparency Order at this point effectively creates a 'black hole' of information which, in some, invites misinterpretation rather than accurate information and debate.*"

- Finally, but with less weight given to it – the humanising factor of a name. The caveat to this was the judge's comment that "*I am not convinced that the story of such extended detention could not be appropriately reported without a name were it not for the extent of the information which is already in the public domain*".

As against lifting the reporting restriction were:

- It is the 'ordinary' approach and there was no evidence that Mr Hickmott had sought publicity himself. Though it was noted that this is just a starting point and "*It would make no sense of having jurisdiction to take another view if it remained determinative*". It was also noted that there was no evidence Mr Hickmott was opposed to publicity and no evidence of past adverse reactions from which inferences could be drawn;

- A "*much weightier factor in favour of anonymity is the risk that granting this application may destabilise Mr Hickmott's current care arrangements and make his future care more difficult to arrange*". However, the judge noted that on the evidence the care provider had provided, she was not persuaded that the risk was that heavy.

Balancing the above considerations the decision was that parts of the transparency order would be disapplied and that Mr Hickmott could be named in reporting about the case.

It would appear from this decision that the public interest in the facts of the matter, in this case the fact that P had been detained for a very lengthy period of time beyond which he was considered fit for discharge from detention, was a factor which carried weight in allowing the matter to be reported.

However, as noted by the judge, this is not an issue which required the naming of P in order to report on it. Rather, the particular facts of P's case, and especially the previous extensive reporting, were clearly crucial in tipping the balance in favour of allowing the reporting of Mr Hickmott's name.

The judge's observation was that given the information already available the likelihood was that much of this was known before the Court of Protection proceedings had started, and would be known afterwards, such that maintaining the transparency order and reporting restrictions would in effect be creating a "*black hole*" of information for the life of the Court of Protection proceedings. This is at odds with the general approach of increasing transparency and openness within Court of Protection proceedings.

Clearly, consideration was given to the risks of harm to P. In particular, the concern that P's care package might be destabilised was a factor which the court weighed carefully. Ultimately however the court was not persuaded that this was a realistic risk based on the evidence before it.

Another case in which the reporting restrictions were lifted is that of *Manchester University NHS Foundation Trust v Verden & Anor [2022]* EWCOP 4 (08 February 2022)[35]

The case concerned William Verden who was aged 17. He suffered from steroid resistant nephrotic syndrome, and at the time of the judgment was in end stage renal failure and needed ongoing dialysis (haemodialysis) or a transplant to stay alive. He had diagnoses of moderate to severe learning difficulties, autism, and ADHD with accompanying behavioural disturbances.

The Hospital Trust opposed a transplant due to concerns that William would not cope with the aftercare required. William's mother thought that it was in his best interests to have a transplant. It was agreed that if a transplant was to take place, then a live kidney donor would be

---

35 https://www.bailii.org/ew/cases/EWCOP/2022/4.html

preferable. William's mother therefore also sought an altruistic kidney donor, as none of William's family had been a match.

A reporting restrictions order (RRO) was made in the case by Mr Justice Cohen when the matter first came before him on 31 December 2021. Mr Justice Cohen was not made aware, nor was the Official Solicitor, that in the four to six weeks before the application was made there had been extensive media coverage of William's situation.

The judge noted that in future the expectation would be that any party applying for an RRO would, except in very unusual cases, set out what media coverage has taken place when making the application for the RRO.

William's mother sought to lift the RRO in order to publicise William's case and hopefully find an altruistic kidney donor.

The judge considered William's views and noted that he had informed the Official Solicitor's representative that he would want publicity if it meant he received a new kidney, although he would not want photographs of himself with lines and tubes attached or pictures taken at home.

The BBC argued that an RRO would be a disproportionate restriction on the Article 10 rights of William's mother and "*There is a great public interest in the story, particularly regarding the way that people with disabilities are treated by the NHS and also because the Court of Protection should be scrutinised in the important decisions that it takes.*" [paragraph 16].

In balancing William's Article 8 rights and the Article 10 rights, the judge noted that William supported a media publicity campaign. This was said to be time sensitive given the need to identify a donor as soon as possible.

In terms of the Article 10 arguments the judge noted: i) the story was already in the public domain and there would not be able to be any publicity of the substantive hearing at all given the risk of jigsaw identification; ii) the public interest in how people with autism are treated by the NHS; and iii) the need to scrutinise the work of the Court of Protection given the crucial life changing decisions the court takes.

The judge noted that any reporting would lead to the identification of William and his family, which the RRO is designed to prevent and that the alternative would be no publicity at all which is not proportionate.

Weight was also given to the desire to find an altruistic donor and therefore to the Article 10 rights relied on by William's mother. The RRO was therefore amended including to allow the identification of William.

It is worth noting that as with the decision in Tony Hickmott's case, a factor that weighed in favour of lifting the RRO was that if the reporting restrictions were not lifted this would in effect mean that no reporting at all would be possible, given the past publicity prior to the proceedings being brought.

Noting the judge's comments, where a reporting restrictions order or transparency order is being sought, the parties will need to ensure that the court is informed of any past reporting on the matter when making that application.

A similar issue arose in the matter of *Norfolk and Norwich University Hospitals NHS Foundation Trust & Ors v Tooke & Ors [2023] EWCOP 45* (20 October 2023)[36].

The case concerned a 29-year-old young man, Jordan Tooke. He had a diagnosis of autism, severe learning disabilities, and William's syndrome, which is characterised by developmental delay and other variable features. He was unable to communicate verbally but "*is effective, indeed dextrous, in non-verbal communication.*" He had been diagnosed as suffering from chronic kidney disease and had now entered end-stage renal failure. His condition had deteriorated and without haemodialysis would die.

It was not thought that he would be able to tolerate haemodialysis, although a plan was made for de-sensitisation work. He was on the transplant list.

Jordan's family were "*intensely committed to promoting the rights of people with disabilities and keen to take opportunity to signal to the wider public the importance of those rights*" [paragraph 37]. The judgment noted "*How society treats some of its weakest and most vulnerable is undoubtedly a measure of its own health and maturity.*" [paragraph 37]. The parents sought the lifting of the RRO to promote those principles.

The judge noted that there were two additional practical considerations which had led him to yield to that application:

- The possibility of finding an altruistic donor; and
- Finding specialist clothing that would assist with dialysis. It being noted "*The central venous catheter (CVC) remains in situ*

36 https://www.bailii.org/ew/cases/EWCOP/2023/45.html

> *permanently throughout dialysis. There is an ever-present risk of Jordan pulling it and perhaps detaching it. His parents have assiduously researched to see whether there is any bespoke clothing that can effectively cover the line to diminish risk of Jordan accidentally or intentionally disconnecting the CVC. They have not been able to identify an operative supplier at the moment*" [paragraph 39]. It was hoped that publicity may assist in this search.

The court revisited the issue of discharging the transparency order in the matter of *VS (deceased), Re* [2024] EWCOP 6 (19 December 2023)[37]. This case concerned an application to lift a transparency order after the death of P, Mr Stephens. Concern was expressed by the daughter of Mr Stephens' partner that allegations had been made about her which were not accurate, and she was concerned about the impact on her personally and professionally if the reporting restrictions were lifted so that those allegations could be discussed publicly.

In deciding that the balance came down "*very heavily*" in favour of lifting the reporting restrictions order, the court noted that Mr Stephens was no longer in need of the protection of the transparency order.

Furthermore, Her Honour Judge Hilder expressed a concern that it was neither the role nor practically possible for the Court of Protection to control the accuracy or fairness of reporting, noting that in any event that was "*not the meaning of freedom of speech*" and that "*The answer to any concerns of 'balance' in reporting is probably more openness, not less*" [paragraph 21].

[37] https://www.bailii.org/ew/cases/EWCOP/2024/6.html

A decision not to lift the reporting restrictions

It is worth contrasting those cases with the court's decision in the matter of *LF v A NHS Trust & Ors* [2022] EWCOP 8 (07 March 2022)[38].

The matter concerned a 27-year-old woman (G), who had a degenerative disorder affecting her central nervous system. Previous decisions had been made by the court in respect of her best interests.

Importantly the judge had determined that it was in G's best interests to leave the children's hospital where she had been residing for many years, and which all agreed was not a suitable placement, and move to a placement 'A' Home. It was agreed that ultimately the intention of the care plan should be to return G to her parents' home, but that she required a full and comprehensive assessment of her needs outside of the hospital setting before this could be progressed.

G's father, LF, made an application to lift the RRO, ostensibly to enable a crowd funding campaign for a specially adapted vehicle to transport G in the community.

What is clear from the judgment is that the judge did not consider this to be the real reason for the father's desire to lift the RRO. His concern was that the father had not accepted his decision that it was in G's best interests to move to 'A' Home. He relied on emails from two press organisations to the Trust seeking information about the case, and which noted that G's parents did not agree with the judge's decision that G should move to 'A' Home.

Concern was raised that the impact on 'A' Home of lifting the RRO would be adverse. The judge was clearly troubled by the prospect of

38 https://www.bailii.org/ew/cases/EWCOP/2022/8.html

this, noting "*it would be devastating if the placement were jeopardised or sabotaged*", and "*What is contemplated is a highly conflictual situation with a confrontational father, ventilating his perceived grievances in the public domain. It is not difficult to see how generating this kind of environment might alienate and undermine the staff at A Care Home to a degree which might cause them either to withdraw from it, or potentially to terminate it.*" [paragraph 16].

The judge confirmed the approach of the earlier case law, i.e. the balancing exercise identified by Lord Steyn in *Re S*, with neither right taking precedence and therefore an evaluation of the evidential weight and the outcome determined by which right establishes qualitatively greater evidence.

Mr Justice Hayden distinguished the case from that of *PH*, in which anonymisation was lifted. The judge noted that G's Article 8 rights were "*manifestly*" engaged, pointing to the fact that the proposed placement in 'A' Home was to enable G's needs to be assessed and thereafter for her to transition to a return to her parents' home "*when and if that was assessed as being in her best interests*" [paragraph 22].

The concern raised by the judge was that if LF's wish of G returning immediately home came to fruition then she would in effect have been "*set up to fail*", given that the evidence supported a placement in 'A' Home at this time.

The case was also said to be "*the polar opposite*" to the William Verden case, because in that case publicity was sought to save William's life but in this case publicity was sought to "*subvert*" the outcome which had been determined to be in G's best interests – "*It follows that in this case, the Article 10 right asserted by the father is to pursue, in the public domain, an outcome which has been assessed as contrary to his daughter's interests*" [paragraph 25].

The competing rights were G's right to be cared for safely in order to maximise the quality of her life, and a central objective to afford her the opportunity of family life in the fullest possible way i.e. returning home if possible, and LF's right to his freedom of speech. In respect of LF's right, the judge noted "*It is not to be curtailed merely because what he wishes to say to the media is, on all the available evidence, misguided, and inaccurate, rather it is because it is in direct conflict with his daughter's rights as I have analysed them*" [paragraph 26]. On that basis the restriction on LF's Article 10 rights was determined to be a proportionate and necessary intervention, although not one that was set in stone.

Summary

Despite the differing outcomes in the cases discussed above what is clear is that P's Article 8 rights, considered through the lens of the analysis of their best interests in respect of the matters before the court, will carry significant weight in the balancing exercise to determine if the transparency or reporting restrictions order should be lifted.

Whilst the Article 8 rights of P are not determinative and must be balanced against the Article 10 rights of those wishing to report on or share information about the proceedings, a restriction on the Article 10 rights was found to be proportionate in the matter of *LF* when the court considered that not imposing such a restriction would be harmful to G and not in her best interests.

There were strong arguments in favour of open justice and the Article 10 arguments in the cases of Tony Hickmott, William Verden and Jordan Tooke, in the former to allow the public to understand the significant impact of the resource constraints which had meant that Mr Hickmott had remained detained for a significant period longer than required, and in the latter two cases to enable an understanding of how those with learning disabilities are treated by the NHS.

In the decisions in William Verden and Jordan Tooke's cases there were, additionally, benefits to both of them in terms of the ability to publicise their cases in the hope of seeking an altruistic kidney donor.

The infringements of their Article 8 rights were minimal, in the context of those cases. Contrastingly, in the decision of *LF*, the court was concerned that the father's application to exercise his Article 10 rights to publicise the case were in actual fact intended to subvert the court's best interests decision making, such that this would ultimately lead to a further infringement of G's Article 8 rights.

The decision in the matter of *VS* makes clear that the primary intention of the reporting restrictions is to protect and safeguard P, such that where P is no longer in need of this protection the balance will lie more heavily in favour of lifting the restrictions.

What is clear from all of the decisions is that the court will carefully approach the balancing exercise, and that this will require consideration on the specific facts of the case.

Practitioners dealing with an application to either impose, amend, or lift a transparency or reporting restrictions order will need to give careful thought to the competing Article 8 and Article 10 rights engaged on the specific facts of the case, and consider the proportionality of any infringement on either right, with regard particularly to the welfare of P.

CHAPTER FIVE

TRANSPARENCY AND PRIVACY IN THE CONTEXT OF COMMITTAL PROCEEDINGS IN THE COURT OF PROTECTION

The Rules

As noted in Chapter 1, Rule 4.1(4) of the Court of Protection Rules ('the Rules') provides that the general rule (i.e. that a hearing in the Court of Protection will be in private) does not apply to hearings for a committal order or writ of sequestration.

Part 21 of the Rules sets out the relevant provisions dealing with applications and proceedings in relation to contempt. The rules for how hearings for contempt are dealt with in the Court of Protection are set out at Rule 21.8.

Rule 21.8(1) directs that unless the court makes a different order, a hearing for contempt proceedings must be heard in public:

> *21.8.—(1) All hearings of contempt proceedings shall, irrespective of the parties' consent, be listed and heard in public unless the court otherwise directs, applying the provisions of paragraph (4).*

It is clear from the rules that the court can hold a contempt hearing in private, but it is evident from the language used in the rules that the court is expected to give careful consideration if it is proposing to do so.

Rule 21.8(2) provides:

> *21.8.—(2) In deciding whether to hold a hearing in private, the court must consider any duty to protect or have regard to a right to freedom of expression which may be affected'.*

Rule 21.8(4) sets out the factors that the court will need to consider in deciding whether to hold a contempt hearing in private. It provides:

> *21.8. —(4) A hearing, or any part of it, must be held in private if, and only to the extent that, the court is satisfied of one or more of the matters set out in sub-paragraphs (a) to (g) and that it is necessary to sit in private to secure the proper administration of justice—*
>
> *(a) publicity would defeat the object of the hearing;*
>
> *(b) it involves matters relating to national security;*
>
> *(c) it involves confidential information (including information relating to personal financial matters) and publicity would damage that confidentiality;*
>
> *(d) a private hearing is necessary to protect the interests of P, a protected party or any child;*
>
> *(e) it is a hearing of an application made without notice and it would be unjust to any respondent for there to be a public hearing;*
>
> *(f) it involves uncontentious matters arising in the administration of the affairs of P or in the administration of P's estate; or*

(g) the court for any other reason considers this to be necessary to secure the proper administration of justice.

The case law

The issues of transparency and reporting restrictions in an application for committal for contempt of court were considered in the matter of *Sunderland City Council v Macpherson (Rev 1)* [2023] EWCOP3 (20 January 2023)[39].

This matter concerned an application to commit the defendant to prison for contempt of court. It was alleged that the defendant had breached the injunctive court orders made in the underlying Court of Protection proceedings, not to publish material from the Court of Protection proceedings on internet sites. It is stated in the judgment that if the defendant published that material it would identify or was likely to identify P, and would publicise details about her condition and treatment.

As is noted in the judgment, there was a lengthy background to the underlying Court of Protection proceedings. The court had already found that whilst in her mother's care, P had deteriorated to such an extent that she required in-patient treatment under detention under the Mental Health Act 1983 (MHA). Given that harm, the Court of Protection had already determined that it was in P's best interests not to return to her mother's care on discharge from MHA detention, but rather that she should be placed in residential care.

39 https://www.bailii.org/ew/cases/EWCOP/2023/3.html

The court noted that it would be very harmful to P if she either had to be detained again under the MHA, or if she lost her specialist placement.

It was stated that the defendant did not accept that her daughter was unwell, and that she held the belief that harm was being caused to her daughter by clinicians treating her for a condition she does not have, including by the administration of medication which she believed was causing the symptoms her daughter experienced.

It was noted that the defendant had been publicising her views, which in addition to videos '*excoriating*' those caring for her daughter and the Court of Protection, also included videos of P which identified her.

In considering the impact of the new Rule 21.8(5) which came into force in January 2023 it was noted that the court could order that the identity of the defendant in the contempt proceedings could be withheld if two conditions were met, firstly that non-disclosure was considered necessary to secure the proper administration of justice and secondly that it was in order to protect the interests of the defendant.

The court recognised that the new Rule 21.8 (5) circumscribed the general power under Rule 4.2 to impose restrictions on the publication of the identity of any party.

It was also noted that Rule 21.8(5) did allow the court to restrict the disclosure of P's identity, but again this would require two conditions to be met. Firstly, that non-disclosure was considered necessary to secure the proper administration of justice and secondly that it was in order to protect the interests of P.

Whilst the judge in this case was unsure whether the rules would permit the restriction of the disclosure of another party's identity in order to secure the administration of justice and to protect the interests of P, he did go on to note that any such order would need to be necessary and proportionate.

It is worth noting the considerations which the judge in that case weighed for and against restricting reporting in the case. These are set out at paragraph 39 of the judgment:

> "*i. Mrs Macpherson is the defendant in contempt of court proceedings that might result in her imprisonment. There is a strong public interest in allowing the press and bloggers to identify the defendant. It may be considered to be harmful to the public's trust in and understanding of the Court of Protection to imprison, or at least to consider the exercise of the power to imprison, a person whose identity is kept secret.*
>
> *ii. FP is a vulnerable person whose interests lie in being protected from invasions of her privacy and publicity about her history, condition, and circumstances.*
>
> *iii. Publicity concerning the Defendant's distorted beliefs and unfounded allegations against those caring for and treating FP, will tend to erode the willingness of those professionals to continue to treat and care for FP. The strain put on healthcare professionals by such allegations should not be under-estimated. Identifying the Defendant will risk amplifying the stream of allegations she makes against the healthcare professionals dealing with her daughter.*
>
> *iv. There is a published judgment which gives details about FP. Allowing the Defendant's identity to be reported will create a substantial risk identifying FP as the subject of that judgment.*

v. The Defendant has used FP's first name in her online posts. She has been ordered to remove those posts but has, before today, failed or refused to do so. Therefore, naming the Defendant in reports of these contempt proceedings will risk allowing FP to be identified as the subject of those posts and of the judgment referred to.

vi. FP and the Defendant have different surnames which mitigates the risk of identification of FP if the Defendant's identity is disclosed.

vii. FP is largely isolated from contact with others. It is unlikely that she will directly encounter any person who has found out her identity, and her connection with the Court of Protection proceedings herein, through reporting of her mother's name as the defendant to the committal application. Even if FP is identified by reason of her mother's name being reported, it is not likely that FP will suffer direct harm as a result."

The decision of the court, balancing these considerations and of course the respective Article 8 and Article 10 rights, and considering the new Part 21 of the Rules, was that the defendant's name could be reported but that reporting of P's identity and her placement would not be permitted.

In the matter of *Re Esper v NHS NW London ICB (Appeal : Anonymity in Committal Proceedings)* (Rev1) [2023] EWCOP 29 (10 July 2023)[40], Mr Justice Poole again considered the issue of reporting restrictions in committal proceedings.

40 https://www.bailii.org/ew/cases/EWCOP/2023/29.html

The first instance judge who heard the contempt proceedings made a reporting restrictions order which ordered that the identity of P and P's other family members should be withheld, but which ordered that the contemnor's identity could be reported. The contemnor appealed that decision.

Within the judgment it was noted that there is a practice direction issued by the Lord Chief Justice in respect of committal for contempt of court dated March 2015: Committal for Contempt of Court – Open Court [2015] 1 WLR 2195[41] (2015 Practice Direction). This practice direction applies to proceedings in the Court of Protection, however it has not been updated and so does not reflect the changes made to Part 21 of the Rules in January 2023.

This has led to inconsistencies between the 2015 Practice Direction and the Court of Protection Rules.

Paragraph 13 of the 2015 Practice Direction makes it a mandatory requirement that a defendant who has committed a contempt of court must be named and their name published.

Rule 21.8(5) of the Rules however requires the court not to disclose the identity of a party (which would thereby include the defendant) if the two tests of necessity within that rule are met.

The first limb of the test is that the non-disclosure of the identity of the party must be necessary to secure the proper administration of justice. The second limb is that the non-disclosure is needed to protect *that person's* interests [own emphasis added]. Paragraphs 39 to 43 of the judgment provide a detailed analysis of the test.

41 https://www.judiciary.uk/wp-content/uploads/2015/03/practice-direction-committals-for-contempt.pdf

Also worth noting from this decision is the judge's observation about the "*narrowness of COPR r21.8(5)*" such that it is important to identify who is a party for the purposes of such an order being made, i.e. to withhold their identify.

It was concluded that applying the requirements under Rule 21.3, which requires a contempt application made in existing proceedings before the Court of Protection to be made by an application under Part 10 *in those proceedings*; and applying the overriding objective at Rule 1.3, in particular the requirement to ensure that P's interests and position is properly considered, those persons who are parties in the Court of Protection proceedings will be the parties in the committal proceedings. As such, Rule 21.8(5) of the Rules may be applied to any of those parties.

A further issue which arose in this case was the fact that the defendant's name had already been included in the listing of the contempt hearing, in accordance with the Rules.

Pending any clarification from the Court of Protection Rules Committee, the judge suggested that every committal application in the Court of Protection should be put before the appropriate judge in advance of the first hearing in the committal proceedings, to determine whether pursuant to Rule 21.8(5) the identification of the defendant's name in the public court list should be prevented. This would require the necessity tests in Rule 21.8(5) to be met and it was suggested that the press should also be notified and given an opportunity to make representations about this issue at the first hearing, before the defendant is publicly identified.

If no such order is made prohibiting the identification of the defendant then their name should appear in the court's list.

As with other judgments considered already in this guide, the court confirmed the fundamental principle of open justice and noted that the general rule is that hearings should be carried out, and judgments and orders made, in public.

It was also observed that it "*will be a rare case in which the two-limb test allowing the court to order non-disclosure of a defendant's identity will be satisfied, and an extremely rare case where they are met in respect of a defendant found to have committed a contempt of court and/or who has been made the subject of a committal order*" [paragraph 36].

Derogations from the general principle can only be justified in exceptional circumstances, when strictly necessary and in order to secure the proper administration of justice.

The matter of *Lincolnshire County Council v X & Ors* [2023] EWCOP 52 (19 July 2023)[42] is an example of a decision in which there was a derogation from the general principle in order to protect P from harm.

Whilst the judgment was published by the court, the decision was that the hearing itself should be in private.

In considering the Official Solicitor's application for the proceedings to be in private, the judge noted that this was a significant application for the court to determine, and that the authorities demonstrate that "*open justice is a fundamental principle in a democratic society, and for good reason.It is a principle which must be closely guarded. Any application to depart from it should be subject to careful consideration, and robust and rigorous scrutiny*" [paragraph 4].

42 https://www.bailii.org/ew/cases/EWCOP/2023/52.html

It was further noted that the principles of open justice apply *"with more potent effect"* in proceedings where an individual's liberty is at risk, which include proceedings for contempt and committal.

The judgment considers the importance of open justice under the European Convention of Human rights, Article 6, but recognises that both the ECHR and national courts have identified exceptions or derogations to the principle of open justice, including in respect of committal hearings being heard in public, although the judge stressed the fact that these are to be an exception.

It was noted that Article 6 allows for a hearing, or part of it, to be heard in private if the court is satisfied that a number of conditions are established, i.e. *"the restriction must be strictly necessary in the special circumstances of the case, where publicity would prejudice the interests of justice; exclusion of the press or public is required in the interests of morals, public order, national security in a democratic society, where the interests of juveniles or the protection of the private life of the parties so require"* [paragraph 12].

The court recognised the need to undertake the balancing exercise as between Article 8 and Article 10, as considered in the previous cases considered in this and earlier chapters.

It was noted that the 2015 Practice Direction made clear that open justice is a fundamental principle, with derogations only being justified in exceptional circumstances, when strictly necessary to secure the proper administration of justice.

It was further noted that the amendments to the Rules, as set out above, make provision for a hearing to be in private only if it is necessary to secure the proper administration of justice and one of the matters in sub-paragraphs (a) to (g) of Rule 21.8(4).

The judgment confirms that in considering whether to exercise its power to hold a hearing in private or to withhold the identity of P or another party or witness, the court must undertake the 'ultimate balancing exercise', consider whether the circumstances in sub-paragraphs (a) to (g) of Rule 21.8(4) apply and, additionally, whether it is necessary to sit in private for the proper administration of justice.

In noting that Rule 21 addresses the principles enshrined by Article 6 in respect of the principle of open justice, in the specific context of the Court of Protection, the judgment emphasised "*The starting point is the principle of open justice. However, when competing interests or rights arise which are so compelling that failing to afford them specific protection risks the proper administration of justice, the Court should consider sitting in private and (according to the express terms of COP 2017 r.21(4)) must do so if satisfied that that that risk arises*" [paragraph 23].

In considering the effect of Rule 21.8(5) the judge took the view that this is a mandatory provision such that if the court is satisfied that non-disclosure of a party or witnesses' identity is necessary to secure the administration of justice; and, secondly, that doing so is necessary to protect the interests of the party or witness, it must order non-disclosure of that person's identity.

Importantly, in deciding whether to sit in private, the court accepted the submission that the court must be satisfied that no lesser measure would be sufficient to protect P and also secure the administration of justice.

The court considered and balanced the principle of open justice, as enshrined in Article 6, against the Article 8 rights of P and the Article 10 rights that would be engaged by any reporting restrictions. Additionally, on the facts of this particular case, the judge also had regard to Article 14 (protection from discrimination) and Article 3 (protection from inhuman or degrading treatment), and potentially

Article 2 (right to life), in light of reports that P had been feeling suicidal as a result of the anxiety caused by the proceedings.

The factors and risks which the court considered in the balance were that there was evidence that P would experience heightened anxiety and distress because of their fear arising from threats made against them by one of the defendants, in addition to the existing distress and anxiety regarding the proceedings. A second concern was that having learned about the proceedings, the defendants' associates may take steps to harm P. The third risk was that private information about P, their life, their experiences of harm and their diagnoses could be seen and read by others.

It was acknowledged that a reporting restrictions order could possibly reduce or ameliorate the second and third concerns, but that it would not be able to address the first concern. The judge stressed that the anxiety went beyond "*simply worry or concern about the proceedings*" and noted that "*It is part of the very harm which the proceedings seek to protect against*".

The judge therefore distinguished the case from that of *McPherson* and *Esper*, and concluded that it was rightly described as exceptional such that the derogation from the principle of open justice by holding the hearing in private was justified on the basis of the test of necessity having been met, in order to meet the interests of justice and effect the proper administration of justice, and to protect P's interests.

It was noted in the judgment that the issue of whether the alleged contemnors should be named was not straightforward. This decision was adjourned for further consideration. It is not clear from subsequent judgments whether this issue was revisited.

Summary

As is noted above the rules in respect of hearings in relation to committal applications are different, and any hearing for a committal application will usually be heard in public.

As noted in the *Lincolnshire* decision there is scope for this usual approach to be derogated from, however the court was very clear that it would expect this to occur in exceptional cases only.

There is scope within the rules for the anonymity of any party to the committal application to be protected by way of an application to withhold their identification in any reporting or judgment, however in the decision in *Esper* and *Lincolnshire* it was made clear that an application for the anonymisation of a defendant to a committal application, and particularly one who has been found to have been in contempt of court, is very unlikely to succeed.

CHAPTER SIX

TRANSPARENCY IN THE CONTEXT OF CLOSED PROCEEDINGS

The guidance

There is now guidance, issued by the then Vice President of the Court of Protection, Mr Justice Hayden, addressing closed material and closed proceedings in the Court of Protection. This is published on Bailii at https://www.bailii.org/ew/cases/EWCOP/2023/6.html. This guidance deals more widely with closed proceedings and closed material, but does touch upon the issue of transparency as dealt with further below.

As explained in the guidance a closed hearing is different from a private hearing. A closed hearing is one in which a party and, if they are represented, their representatives are excluded. Whereas a private hearing is one which all parties attend but from which the press and public are excluded.

Dealing with transparency, the guidance confirms that the expectation is that a closed hearing will fall outside the usual provisions in PD 4C, and that it should therefore be heard in private. It is noted in the guidance that given the very limited circumstances in which the court can order a hearing to be closed, it is very likely that enabling public access would defeat the purpose of the hearing.

The guidance also provides that the requirements of open justice "*still weigh heavily*" such that the court must publish a reasoned judgment at the earliest opportunity that both explains the rationale for holding a closed hearing and the substantive decision of the court.

The case law

This guidance was issued following the decision in the matter of *A (Covert Medication: Closed Proceedings)* [2022] EWCOP 44 (07 October 2022)[43].

The case concerned A, a 23-year old woman who had been found to lack capacity to conduct the litigation or to make decisions about her residence, care, contact with others, and her medical treatment for epilepsy, primary ovarian failure, and vitamin D deficiency.

A had lived at home with her mother, B, until 2019. A had diagnoses of mild learning disability and Asperger's syndrome, epilepsy, primary ovarian failure, and a vitamin D deficiency. A's primary ovarian failure had not been referred to health professionals and so had not been investigated, and so she had not undergone puberty. The court heard evidence from a consultant endocrinologist who confirmed that the advised treatment was hormone therapy which was "*straightforward, guaranteed to succeed, and would transform A from a child to a woman*". Without this treatment the prognosis for A was "*extremely bleak*", with physical and mental health risks.

A was opposed to the treatment, and B had not sought any intervention in relation to the primary ovarian failure. B told the court that she would encourage A to take her medication however it was noted that she had not previously done so. The judge concluded that

[43] https://www.bailii.org/ew/cases/EWCOP/2022/44.html

they had no confidence that B would encourage or support A to take her medication if she remained at home.

The court therefore found that it was in A's best interests to live at placement A, away from B's influence, and to receive treatment for her primary ovarian failure and vitamin D deficiency. Restrictions were placed on the contact between A and B.

A moved to placement A however after a period of time the court remained concerned about B's influence on A and so suspended all contact between them.

The court then held a closed hearing to hear an application from the NHS Trust to medicate A covertly to treat her primary ovarian failure. A decision was made to approve a plan for the covert medication of A.

That plan was then reviewed over a series of closed hearings between 2020 and 2022.

A continued to reside in placement A and had only indirect telephone contact with her mother, who remained unaware of the covert medication.

Separate public hearings took place in respect of the other welfare decisions in this matter. Decisions had been taken in the open hearings about A's residence and care (outside of the treatment), and observers had been present at those hearings, who had then published blogs about the proceedings.

In these blogs, they had expressed concerns that between 2020 and 2022 nothing had been done to resolve the issue of where A should live. It was noted by the observers that A had expressed a wish to return home to live with her mother but that she was being kept from doing so supposedly in order to receive endocrine treatment which it was said she would not be able to receive at home due to her mother's opposition of it, but which had not been progressed in the intervening two years.[44]

A hearing on 15 September 2022 was held in private and was closed, but specifically considered whether the proceedings should remain closed.

Having determined that it was in A's best interests to continue to be given medication covertly, and that B should be told that A was receiving medication covertly, the court determined that the use of closed proceedings could no longer be justified.

It therefore fell to be considered whether the fact that A was and had been medicated covertly should be the subject of a reporting restrictions order.

It was noted that any reporting at all would likely lead to the identification of A by anyone who knew her, given the unique circumstances of her case. As such it was recognised that careful consideration needed to be given to those risks and the risks of A therefore learning about the covert medication.

The court therefore made a reporting restrictions order within the closed proceedings on 15 September 2022. This would remain in effect at the outset of the open hearing on 20 September 2022, in order to ensure that A did not become aware of the covert medication

---

44 As is noted at paragraph 8 of the judgment, the Open Justice Court of Protection Project published its online blog about the case on 2 May 2022. The link to the full blog, titled Medical treatment, undue influence and delayed puberty: A baffling case, by Celia Kitzinger and Claire Martin can be found here: https://openjusticecourtofprotection.org/2022/05/02/medical-treatment-undue-influence-and-delayed-puberty-a-baffling-case/

in an unplanned way given the potentially harmful consequences for her.

In the judgment from the hearing on 20 September 2022, the court noted that notice of the reporting restrictions order was given to the accredited press via the CopyDirect service. No press attended the hearing, but the court did hear submissions from legal bloggers, and noted in particular their concern that the open and closed proceedings running in tandem had led to them inadvertently misleading their readers.[45]

As is noted in the decision, both the NHS Trust and the Official Solicitor supported the lifting of the reporting restrictions order, on the basis that there was considerable public interest in the workings of the Court of Protection. They also noted that there would be a particular interest in decisions that had been made in closed proceedings about covert medication.

Noting the competing rights engaged in the balancing exercise, i.e. Article 8 and Article 10, the court concluded that A's article 8 rights were engaged given the need to protect her physical and mental health. It was noted that in this case it was arguable that A's Article 2 rights might also be engaged, given that she had in the past refused to eat and drink and there was a possibility that she may do so again in response to discovering that those caring for her had been covertly medicating her.

---

45 A statement by the Open Justice Court of Protection published following the hearing regarding the misleading blog posts can be found here: https://openjusticecourtofprotection.org/2022/10/11/statement-from-the-open-justice-court-of-protection-project-concerning-an-inaccurate-and-misleading-blog-post/

The use of covert medication, in this case, was considered to enhance her Article 8 right to develop physically and mentally in a healthy manner.

It was stated that if the reporting restriction order was continued, this would mean that the misleading impression from the blogs relating to the open proceedings would remain uncorrected, i.e. that A has been kept away from her mother on the basis that she was to receive treatment, but that this treatment had not been administered.

The court noted that the transparency order now in place would offer protection against A being identified and therefore learning about the covert medication in an unplanned way, as would the injunctions made by the court prohibiting B from discussing the covert medication with A.

The consideration therefore was whether the reporting restrictions remained necessary to prevent either A or anyone she knew learning about the covert medication via reporting on the case.

Consideration was given to the fact that A's case was almost unique, but it was also acknowledged that she had limited contact with only a few family members and that they had not to date queried A having now gone through puberty. Additionally, it was noted that A herself had limited contact with the outside world.

Considering the competing Article 10 rights, the court noted the considerable public interest in a case in the Court of Protection which had involved closed proceedings, with family members being excluded and the use of covert medication to induce puberty in P.

It was also acknowledged that now that B was aware of the covert medication, this placed the issue squarely at the heart of the proceedings as a whole, such that any reporting restrictions on the use of covert medication would in effect be to impose a reporting ban.

Weighing the slim chance of A discovering from any reporting that she had been medicated covertly against the importance of open justice, the decision was that the reporting restrictions order should be discharged. Protections remained in place in the form of the transparency order and the injunctions against B preventing her from informing A that she had been medicated covertly.

One other issue flagged by the court, was that the matter had not even been able to be listed, given that the case number would have alerted A's mother, B, to the existence of the closed proceedings. It was noted that in retrospect, the matter could have been listed without a case number or alternatively with a new case number created specifically for the closed hearings and to make a reporting restrictions order at the outset of the hearing to limit reporting linking the open and closed hearings.

Summary

It is clear from the guidance issued by the Vice President in respect of closed proceedings and hearings that it is anticipated that if closed proceedings are deemed appropriate, then it is unlikely to be considered suitable to allow attendance at such a hearing by the press or the public, nor will it be suitable to hold the hearing in public.

The guidance emphasises however the importance of open justice, which is a theme that is evident across all of the case law considered in this guide, such that the expectation is that a judgment will be published as soon as possible following any closed hearing.

The analysis in the case of *A*, considered above, shows the careful balancing exercise as between P's Article 8 rights and the competing Article 10 rights.

Whilst it was acknowledged that there was a risk that A may discover that she had been covertly medicated, this risk was considered to be slim, and the court clearly took the view that there was significant weight in the Article 10 rights and the need for the public to understand decisions of this nature, where P had been medicated covertly and against their wishes.

CHAPTER SEVEN

CONCLUSIONS

The usual position is now that proceedings in the Court of Protection will be heard in public, but subject to a transparency order made under Rule 4.3 of the Court of Protection Rules (the Rules). This has been the 'ordinary' position since December 2017 and the introduction of Practice Direction 4C – Transparency (PD 4C).

The court retains the power, by virtue of the general rule in Rule 4.1 of the Rules, to hold a hearing or part of a hearing in private. The court also has the power to permit attendance to all or part of a private hearing, and to make orders restricting the information from a hearing which is heard in private but to which permission is given to attend.

When considering whether to hold all or part of a hearing in private, the court should have regard to the factors set out in paragraph 2.5 of PD 4C. The court also has to balance the competing convention rights of P, in terms of their Article 8 rights, and the Article 10 rights of the press and public who might wish to report and publish information about the proceedings.

Consideration is given by the court to the nature of the information which is before it, acknowledging that this will often be personal, private and deeply sensitive to P. Often, P will not have instigated proceedings, or have had any control over the matter coming to court, and it is likely that they will not have the mental capacity to consent to their information being shared.

In balancing the competing rights, the court will undertake a *Re S* balancing exercise of the Article 8 and Article 10 rights, with neither right taking precedence and the court therefore needing to consider on the specific facts of the case the proportionality of the interference with each right.

It is clear from the decisions considered in earlier chapters that significant weight is given to the Article 10 arguments and that any interference with those rights will need to be justified by the specific facts of the case.

However, whilst the court will attempt to give effect to the important principle of open justice, this is not done at the expense of P's rights. Consideration must be given to the risks of harm to P from the disclosure of their private information.

As is shown by the case law, the court will take steps to ensure that P is protected from harm in any decision about whether the proceedings will be private or public, and the information that can be reported. The possible risks to P are a significant factor in the court's decision-making in this regard.

Measures can be taken short of hearing proceedings in public, for example making an order to permit attendance at a private hearing by accredited members of the press and/or publishing an anonymised judgment.

The case law, however, makes it clear that this will be the exception and that the presumption should now be for hearings in the Court of Protection to be heard in public unless there are strong countervailing factors for doing so.

If proceedings are being heard in public, the court will ordinarily make a transparency order to set out any restrictions on the information that can be reported. Although there is a standard template for such orders, there may be information specific to the individual case which should not be reported, particularly if this would result in jigsaw identification of P or if the material may cause distress to P if they become aware that it is in the public domain.

Consideration should be given on a case-by-case basis as to what information may need to be restricted from publication.

The transparency order may also include restrictions on the identification of P's family members, as well as professionals involved in the care and treatment of P. In respect of family members, this is usually to prevent the jigsaw identification of P. In respect of professionals caring for P, the case law makes clear that primarily this is to ensure that P's care is not impacted by this information being published.

It is clear, from the decision in *ST*, that where there may be an infringement of the Article 8 rights of those whose identity is sought to be reported, for example clinicians and those treating P, consideration will be given to the impact on their Article 8 rights. Although it is also clear that this is unlikely to result in indefinite anonymity orders, but rather the court may consider it proportionate to allow some time for any tensions to dissipate before their identities can be reported.

The decision in *Kent County Council v P & Anor* makes it clear that a live criminal investigation may be a countervailing factor against lifting the reporting restrictions or hearing proceedings in public, but it will not be determinative of that decision.

As is shown by the case law in which all reporting restrictions have been lifted, the court will also carry out the *Re S* balancing exercise in respect of that decision as well. The decision will be case and fact specific, however factors which have weighed in favour of disapplying or varying the transparency order or reporting restrictions order have included: i) where there has been a significant amount of information in the public domain before the case has come before the Court of Protection, meaning that any reporting would risk jigsaw identification, and that this would in effect prevent any reporting at all on the case, and ii) if P themselves supports this.

Factors which the court has considered would go against the varying or disapplication of the reporting restrictions have been if there is a risk of harm to P, whether through them being distressed by any reporting or if this might risk the stability of their placement or care arrangements.

Practitioners will need to give careful thought to the competing Article 8 and 10 rights when making an application to impose any sort of reporting restrictions, having regard to the specific facts of the case and the proportionality of any infringement of either right.

In respect of applications in relation to proceedings for contempt of court, the general rule that proceedings are in private is disapplied by Part 21 of the Court of Protection Rules. Part 21 requires that these proceedings are held in public.

Provision is made for the identity of the defendant, other parties, and also P to be anonymised however this is subject to the two-limb test set out at Part 21 of the Rules and is specific to each person whose identity is sought to be anonymised. The two-limb test requires that non-disclosure of the identity of the party must be necessary to secure the proper administration of justice, and secondly that non-disclosure is needed to protect *that person's* interests [own emphasis added].

What is clear from the case law in relation to proceedings in respect of a contempt of court is that open justice remains a fundamental principle and that any derogation from this would need to be exceptional.

In relation to closed proceedings in the Court of Protection, it is acknowledged by the court that these are likely to require that the proceedings are heard in private. However, the guidance on closed hearings and proceedings makes it clear that the court is still expected to give a reasoned judgment at the earliest opportunity, which explains the rationale for the closed hearing and also any substantive decisions which the court has made within that closed hearing.

Open justice is a fundamental principle which the Court of Protection will seek to give effect to wherever possible, provided that this will not cause harm to P.

The relevant principles that are applied in balancing the Article 8 rights of P as against the Article 10 rights of the wider public are well established.

However, the practice of hearings now generally now being heard in public in the Court of Protection, following the introduction of PD 4C, is relatively recent. As the various cases discussed in the guide have shown, the court has continued to grapple with new issues which have arisen as a result of this shift.

The Rules Committee is understood to be reviewing the standard wording of the template transparency order, and therefore there may be further developments in that regard in due course.

MORE BOOKS BY LAW BRIEF PUBLISHING

A selection of our other titles available now:-

'A Practical Guide to the Independent School Standards – September 2023 Edition' by Sarah McKimm
'A Practical Guide to Estate Administration and Crypto Assets' by Richard Marshall
'A Practical Guide to Managing GDPR Data Subject Access Requests – Second Edition' by Patrick O'Kane
'A Practical Guide to Parental Alienation in Private and Public Law Children Cases' by Sam King QC & Frankie Shama
'Contested Heritage – Removing Art from Land and Historic Buildings' by Richard Harwood QC, Catherine Dobson, David Sawtell
'The Limits of Separate Legal Personality: When Those Running a Company Can Be Held Personally Liable for Losses Caused to Third Parties Outside of the Company' by Dr Mike Wilkinson
'A Practical Guide to Transgender Law' by Robin Moira White & Nicola Newbegin
'A Practical Guide to 'Stranded Spouses' in Family Law' by Mani Singh Basi
'A Practical Guide to Residential Freehold Conveyancing' by Lorraine Richardson
'A Practical Guide to Pensions on Divorce for Lawyers' by Bryan Scant
'A Practical Guide to Challenging Sham Marriage Allegations in Immigration Law' by Priya Solanki
'A Practical Guide to Digital Communications Evidence in Criminal Law' by Sam Willis
'A Practical Guide to Legal Rights in Scotland' by Sarah-Jane Macdonald
'A Practical Guide to New Build Conveyancing' by Paul Sams & Rebecca East
'A Practical Guide to Defending Barristers in Disciplinary Cases' by Marc Beaumont
'A Practical Guide to Inherited Wealth on Divorce' by Hayley Trim
'A Practical Guide to Practice Direction 12J and Domestic Abuse in Private Law Children Proceedings' by Rebecca Cross & Malvika Jaganmohan

'A Practical Guide to Confiscation and Restraint' by Narita Bahra QC, John Carl Townsend, David Winch
'A Practical Guide to the Law of Forests in Scotland' by Philip Buchan
'A Practical Guide to Health and Medical Cases in Immigration Law' by Rebecca Chapman & Miranda Butler
'A Practical Guide to Bad Character Evidence for Criminal Practitioners by Aparna Rao
'A Practical Guide to Extradition Law post-Brexit' by Myles Grandison et al
'A Practical Guide to Hoarding and Mental Health for Housing Lawyers' by Rachel Coyle
'A Practical Guide to Psychiatric Claims in Personal Injury – 2nd Edition' by Liam Ryan
'Stephens on Contractual Indemnities' by Richard Stephens
'A Practical Guide to the EU Succession Regulation' by Richard Frimston
'A Practical Guide to Solicitor and Client Costs – 2nd Edition' by Robin Dunne
'Constructive Dismissal – Practice Pointers and Principles' by Benjimin Burgher
'A Practical Guide to Religion and Belief Discrimination Claims in the Workplace' by Kashif Ali
'A Practical Guide to the Law of Medical Treatment Decisions' by Ben Troke
'Fundamental Dishonesty and QOCS in Personal Injury Proceedings: Law and Practice' by Jake Rowley
'A Practical Guide to the Law in Relation to School Exclusions' by Charlotte Hadfield & Alice de Coverley
'A Practical Guide to Divorce for the Silver Separators' by Karin Walker
'The Right to be Forgotten – The Law and Practical Issues' by Melissa Stock
'A Practical Guide to Planning Law and Rights of Way in National Parks, the Broads and AONBs' by James Maurici QC, James Neill et al
'A Practical Guide to Election Law' by Tom Tabori
'A Practical Guide to the Law in Relation to Surrogacy' by Andrew Powell
'A Practical Guide to Claims Arising from Fatal Accidents – 2nd Edition' by James Patience
'A Practical Guide to the Ownership of Employee Inventions – From Entitlement to Compensation' by James Tumbridge & Ashley Roughton
'A Practical Guide to Asbestos Claims' by Jonathan Owen & Gareth McAloon

'A Practical Guide to Stamp Duty Land Tax in England and Northern Ireland' by Suzanne O'Hara
'A Practical Guide to the Law of Farming Partnerships' by Philip Whitcomb
'Covid-19, Homeworking and the Law – The Essential Guide to Employment and GDPR Issues' by Forbes Solicitors
'Covid-19 and Criminal Law – The Essential Guide' by Ramya Nagesh
'Covid-19 and Family Law in England and Wales – The Essential Guide' by Safda Mahmood
'A Practical Guide to the Law of Unlawful Eviction and Harassment – 2nd Edition' by Stephanie Lovegrove
'Covid-19, Brexit and the Law of Commercial Leases – The Essential Guide' by Mark Shelton
'A Practical Guide to Costs in Personal Injury Claims – 2nd Edition' by Matthew Hoe
'A Practical Guide to the General Data Protection Regulation (GDPR) – 2nd Edition' by Keith Markham
'Ellis on Credit Hire – Sixth Edition' by Aidan Ellis & Tim Kevan
'A Practical Guide to Working with Litigants in Person and McKenzie Friends in Family Cases' by Stuart Barlow
'Protecting Unregistered Brands: A Practical Guide to the Law of Passing Off' by Lorna Brazell
'A Practical Guide to Secondary Liability and Joint Enterprise Post-Jogee' by Joanne Cecil & James Mehigan
'A Practical Guide to the Pre-Action RTA Claims Protocol for Personal Injury Lawyers' by Antonia Ford
'A Practical Guide to Neighbour Disputes and the Law' by Alexander Walsh
'A Practical Guide to Forfeiture of Leases' by Mark Shelton
'A Practical Guide to Coercive Control for Legal Practitioners and Victims' by Rachel Horman
'A Practical Guide to the Law of Driverless Cars – Second Edition' by Alex Glassbrook, Emma Northey & Scarlett Milligan
'A Practical Guide to TOLATA Claims' by Greg Williams
'A Practical Guide to Elderly Law – 2nd Edition' by Justin Patten
'A Practical Guide to Responding to Housing Disrepair and Unfitness Claims' by Iain Wightwick

'A Practical Guide to the Law of Bullying and Harassment in the Workplace' by Philip Hyland

'How to Be a Freelance Solicitor: A Practical Guide to the SRA-Regulated Freelance Solicitor Model' by Paul Bennett

'A Practical Guide to Prison Injury Claims' by Malcolm Johnson

'A Practical Guide to the Small Claims Track – 2nd Edition' by Dominic Bright

'A Practical Guide to Advising Clients at the Police Station' by Colin Stephen McKeown-Beaumont

'A Practical Guide to Antisocial Behaviour Injunctions' by Iain Wightwick

'Practical Mediation: A Guide for Mediators, Advocates, Advisers, Lawyers, and Students in Civil, Commercial, Business, Property, Workplace, and Employment Cases' by Jonathan Dingle with John Sephton

'The Mini-Pupillage Workbook' by David Boyle

'A Practical Guide to Crofting Law' by Brian Inkster

'A Practical Guide to the Law of Domain Names and Cybersquatting' by Andrew Clemson

'A Practical Guide to the Law of Gender Pay Gap Reporting' by Harini Iyengar

'NHS Whistleblowing and the Law' by Joseph England

'Employment Law and the Gig Economy' by Nigel Mackay & Annie Powell

'A Practical Guide to Noise Induced Hearing Loss (NIHL) Claims' by Andrew Mckie, Ian Skeate, Gareth McAloon

'An Introduction to Beauty Negligence Claims – A Practical Guide for the Personal Injury Practitioner' by Greg Almond

'Intercompany Agreements for Transfer Pricing Compliance' by Paul Sutton

'Zen and the Art of Mediation' by Martin Plowman

'A Practical Guide to the SRA Principles, Individual and Law Firm Codes of Conduct 2019 – What Every Law Firm Needs to Know' by Paul Bennett

'A Practical Guide to Adoption for Family Lawyers' by Graham Pegg

'A Practical Guide to Industrial Disease Claims' by Andrew Mckie & Ian Skeate

'A Practical Guide to Conducting a Sheriff Court Proof' by Andrew Stevenson

'A Practical Guide to Vicarious Liability' by Mariel Irvine

'A Practical Guide to Applications for Landlord's Consent and Variation of Leases' by Mark Shelton

'A Practical Guide to Relief from Sanctions Post-Mitchell and Denton' by Peter Causton

'A Practical Guide to Equity Release for Advisors' by Paul Sams
'A Practical Guide to Financial Services Claims' by Chris Hegarty
'The Law of Houses in Multiple Occupation: A Practical Guide to HMO Proceedings' by Julian Hunt
'Occupiers, Highways and Defective Premises Claims: A Practical Guide Post-Jackson – 2nd Edition' by Andrew Mckie
'A Practical Guide to Financial Ombudsman Service Claims' by Adam Temple & Robert Scrivenor
'A Practical Guide to Running Housing Disrepair and Cavity Wall Claims: 2nd Edition' by Andrew Mckie & Ian Skeate
'A Practical Guide to Holiday Sickness Claims – 2nd Edition' by Andrew Mckie & Ian Skeate
'Arguments and Tactics for Personal Injury and Clinical Negligence Claims' by Dorian Williams
'A Practical Guide to Drone Law' by Rufus Ballaster, Andrew Firman, Eleanor Clot
'A Practical Guide to Compliance for Personal Injury Firms Working With Claims Management Companies' by Paul Bennett
'RTA Allegations of Fraud in a Post-Jackson Era: The Handbook – 2nd Edition' by Andrew Mckie
'RTA Personal Injury Claims: A Practical Guide Post-Jackson' by Andrew Mckie
'On Experts: CPR35 for Lawyers and Experts' by David Boyle
'An Introduction to Personal Injury Law' by David Boyle

These books and more are available to order online direct from the publisher at www.lawbriefpublishing.com, where you can also read free sample chapters. For any queries, contact us on 0844 587 2383 or mail@lawbriefpublishing.com.

Our books are also usually in stock at www.amazon.co.uk with free next day delivery for Prime members, and at good legal bookshops such as Wildy & Sons.

We are regularly launching new books in our series of practical day-to-day practitioners' guides. Visit our website and join our free newsletter to be kept informed and to receive special offers, free chapters, etc.

You can also follow us on Twitter at www.twitter.com/lawbriefpub.

www.ingramcontent.com/pod-product-compliance
Lightning Source LLC
LaVergne TN
LVHW022114200926
848481LV00003B/1171
9781916698420